On the Mysteries
&
On Repentance

St. Ambrose of Milan

Edited by Paul A. Böer, Sr.

VERITATIS SPLENDOR PUBLICATIONS

et cognoscetis veritatem et veritas liberabit vos (Jn 8:32)

MMXIV

Cover Art
VIVARINI, Bartolomeo
St Ambrose Polyptych (detail)
1477
Tempera on wood
Gallerie dell'Accademia, Venice

The text of this book is excerpted from:

A Select Library of the Nicene and Post-Nicene Fathers of the Christian Church, ed. Philip Schaff, LL.D. (Buffalo: The Christian Literature Co., 1887). Vol. X Ambrose: Select Works and Letters.

AD MAJOREM DEI GLORIAM

A SELECT LIBRARY
OF THE
NICENE AND
POST-NICENE FATHERS
OF
THE CHRISTIAN CHURCH.
SECOND SERIES

TRANSLATED INTO ENGLISH WITH PROLEGOMENA AND
EXPLANATORY NOTES.
Edited by
PHILIP SCHAFF, D.D., LL.D.,
PROFESSOR OF CHURCH HISTORY IN THE UNION
THEOLOGICAL SEMINARY, NEW YORK.
AND
HENRY WACE, D.D.,
PRINCIPAL OF KING'S COLLEGE, LONDON.

VOLUME X
Ambrose: Select Works and Letters

T&T CLARK
EDINBURGH

WM. B. EERDMANS PUBLISHING COMPANY
GRAND RAPIDS, MICHIGAN

SOME OF
THE PRINCIPAL WORKS OF ST. AMBROSE,
TRANSLATED
BY
THE REV. H. DE ROMESTIN, M.A.
OF ST. JOHN'S COLLEGE, AND RECTOR OF TIPTREE, ESSEX,
WITH THE ASSISTANCE OF
THE REV. E. DE ROMESTIN, M.A.
OF NEW COLLEGE, OXFORD,
AND
THE REV. H. T. F. DUCKWORTH, M.A.
OF MERTON COLLEGE, OXFORD.

CONTENTS

The Book Concerning the Mysteries. [2829]

Introduction.

The writer explains in the commencement of this treatise that his object was to set forth, for the benefit of those about to be baptized, the rites and meaning of that Sacrament, as well as of Confirmation and the Holy Eucharist. For all these matters were treated with the greatest reserve in the Early Church, for fear of profanation by the heathen, and it was the custom, as in the case of the well-known Catechetical Lectures of St. Cyril of Jerusalem, to explain them to the catechumens during the latter part of Lent.

Treatises of this kind possess therefore a special interest, as in them we find clearly stated the full teaching of the Church at the time when those addresses which have come down to our times were drawn up.

St. Ambrose goes through and explains the greater part, first of the rites usual at the time of solemn baptism, pointing out the deep truths and mysteries underlying these outward things. He then treats Confirmation, referring to the seven gifts of the Holy Spirit; and lastly, speaks of the Holy Eucharist, especially setting forth the doctrine of the Real Presence.

Some writers in and since the sixteenth century have endeavoured to prove that this treatise has been falsely attributed to St. Ambrose, but there can be no real doubt on the matter, as is conclusively shown by the Benedictine Editors, and now universally admitted. The treatise was composed for use during Lent, but in what year cannot be fixed, possibly, from reference made to the treatise De Patriarchis, about a.d. 387.

Chapter I.

St. Ambrose states that after the explanations he has already given of holy living, he will now explain the Mysteries. Then after giving his reasons for not having done so before, he explains the mystery of the opening of the ears, and shows how this was of old done by Christ Himself.

1. We have spoken daily upon subjects connected with morals, when the deeds of the Patriarchs or the precepts of the Proverbs were being read, in order that being taught and instructed by these you might grow accustomed to enter the ways of the ancients and to walk in their paths, and obey the divine commands; in order that being renewed by baptism you might hold to that manner of life which beseems those who are washed.

2. The season now warns us to speak of the Mysteries, and to set forth the purport of the sacraments, which if we had thought it well to teach before baptism to those who were not yet initiated, we should be considered rather to have betrayed than to have portrayed the Mysteries. And then, too, another reason is that the light itself of the Mysteries will shed itself with more effect upon those who are expecting they know not what, than if any discourse had come beforehand.

3. Open, then, your ears, inhale the good savour of eternal life which has been breathed upon you by the grace of the sacraments; which was signified to you by us, when, celebrating the mystery of the

opening, [2830] we said, "Epphatha, which is, Be opened," [2831] that whosoever was coming in quest of peace might know what he was asked, and be bound to remember what he answered.

4. Christ made use of this mystery in the Gospel, as we read, when He healed him who was deaf and dumb. But He touched the mouth, because he who was healed was dumb and was a man, as regards one point that he might open his mouth with the sound of the voice given to him; as regards the other point because that touch was seemly towards a man, but would have been unseemly towards a woman.

[2829] It must be borne in mind that the name Mysteries was that by which the sacraments were commonly known in the Early Church, as it is at the present day in the Greek Church the equivalent of our word sacraments. Of course the word has also its usual wider signification.

[2830] This "opening" was a symbolical act, as is explained in the next section. The celebrant moistened his finger with spittle, wherewith he then touched the ear of the catechumen, saying, "Epphatha."

[2831] S. Mark vii. 34.

Chapter II.
What those who were to be initiated promised on entering the Church, of the witnesses to these promises, and wherefore they then turned themselves to the East.

5. After this the Holy of holies [2832] was opened to you, you entered the sanctuary of regeneration; recall what you were asked, and remember what you answered. You renounced the devil and his works, the world with its luxury and pleasures. That utterance of yours is preserved not in the tombs of the dead, but in the book of the living.

6. You saw there the deacon, you saw the priest, you saw the chief priest [i.e. the bishop]. Consider not the bodily forms, but

the grace of the Mysteries. You spoke in the presence of the angels, as it is written: "For the priest's lips keep knowledge, and they seek the law at his mouth, for he is the angel of the Lord Almighty." [2833] There is no place for deception nor for denial. He is an angel who proclaims the kingdom of Christ and eternal life. He is to be esteemed by you not according to his appearance, but according to his office. Consider what he delivered, reflect upon the rule of life he gave you, recognize his position.

7. You entered, then, that you might discern your adversary, whom you were to renounce as it were to his face, then you turned to the east; for he who renounces the devil turns to Christ, and beholds Him face to face.

 [2832] "Holy of holies," a figurative name given to the baptistery. Comp. St. Cyril of Jerusalem, Cat. Lect. XIX. 11; and with this whole treatise the last four Catechetical Lectures of St. Cyril of Jerusalem in this series, Vol. VII. p. 144 ff.

[2833] Mal. ii. 7.

Chapter III.
St. Ambrose points out that we must consider the divine presence and working in the water and the sacred ministers, and then brings forward many Old Testament figures of baptism.

8. What did you see? Water, certainly, but not water alone; you saw the deacons ministering there, and the bishop asking questions and hallowing. First of all, the Apostle taught you that those things are not to be considered "which we see, but the things which are not seen, for the things which are seen are temporal, but the things which are not seen are eternal." [2834]

For you read elsewhere: "That the invisible things of God, since the creation of the world, are understood through those things which have been made; His eternal power also and Godhead are estimated by His works." [2835] Wherefore also the Lord Himself says: "If ye believe not Me, believe at least the works." [2836] Believe, then, that the presence of the Godhead is there. Do you believe the working, and not believe the presence? Whence should the working proceed unless the presence went before?

9. Consider, however, how ancient is the mystery prefigured even in the origin of the world itself. In the very beginning, when God made the heaven and the earth, "the Spirit," it is said, "moved upon the waters." [2837] He Who was moving upon the waters, was He not working upon the waters? But why should I say, "working"? As regards His presence He was moving. Was He not working Who was moving? Recognize that He was working in that making of the world, when the prophet says: "By the word of the Lord were the heavens made, and all their strength by the spirit of His mouth." [2838] Each statement rests upon the testimony of the prophet, both that He was moving and that He was working. Moses says that He was moving, David testifies that he was working.

10. Take another testimony. All flesh was corrupt by its iniquities. "My Spirit," says God, "shall not remain among men, because they are flesh." [2839] Whereby God shows that the grace of the Spirit is turned away by carnal impurity and the pollution of grave sin. Upon which, God, willing to restore what was lacking, sent the flood and bade just Noah go up into the ark. And he, after having, as the flood was passing off, sent forth first a raven which did not return, sent forth a dove which is said to have returned with an olive twig. [2840] You see the

water, you see the wood [of the ark], you see the dove, and do you hesitate as to the mystery?

11. The water, then, is that in which the flesh is dipped, that all carnal sin may be washed away. All wickedness is there buried. The wood is that on which the Lord Jesus was fastened when He suffered for us. The dove is that in the form of which the Holy Spirit descended, as you have read in the New Testament, Who inspires in you peace of soul and tranquillity of mind. The raven is the figure of sin, which goes forth and does not return, if, in you, too, inwardly and outwardly righteousness be preserved.

12. There is also a third testimony, as the Apostle teaches us: "For all our fathers were under the cloud, and all passed through the sea, and were all baptized to Moses in the cloud and in the sea." [2841] And further, Moses himself says in his song: "Thou sentest Thy Spirit, and the sea covered them." [2842] You observe that even then holy baptism was prefigured in that passage of the Hebrews, wherein the Egyptian perished, the Hebrew escaped. For what else are we daily taught in this sacrament but that guilt is swallowed up and error done away, but that virtue and innocence remain unharmed?

13. You hear that our fathers were under the cloud, and that a kindly cloud, which cooled the heat of carnal passions. That kindly cloud overshadows those whom the Holy Spirit visits. At last it came upon the Virgin Mary, and the Power of the Highest overshadowed her, [2843] when she conceived Redemption for the race of men. And that miracle was wrought in a figure through Moses. If, then, the Spirit was in the figure, is He not present in the reality, since Scripture says to us: "For

the law was given by Moses, but grace and truth came by Jesus Christ." [2844]

14. Marah was a fountain of most bitter water: Moses cast wood into it and it became sweet. [2845] For water without the preaching of the Cross of the Lord is of no avail for future salvation, but, after it has been consecrated by the mystery of the saving cross, it is made suitable for the use of the spiritual laver and of the cup of salvation. As, then, Moses, that is, the prophet, cast wood into that fountain, so, too, the priest utters over this font the proclamation of the Lord's cross, and the water is made sweet for the purpose of grace.

15. You must not trust, then, wholly to your bodily eyes; that which is not seen is more really seen, for the object of sight is temporal, but that other eternal, which is not apprehended by the eye, but is discerned by the mind and spirit.

16. Lastly, let the lessons lately gone through from the Kings teach you. Naaman was a Syrian, and suffered from leprosy, nor could he be cleansed by any. Then a maiden from among the captives said that there was a prophet in Israel, who could cleanse him from the defilement of the leprosy. And it is said that, having taken silver and gold, he went to the king of Israel. And he, when he heard the cause of his coming, rent his clothes, saying, that occasion was rather being sought against him, since things were asked of him which pertained not to the power of kings. Elisha, however, sent word to the king, that he should send the Syrian to him, that he might know there was a God in Israel. And when he had come, he bade him dip himself seven times in the river Jordan.

17. Then he began to reason with himself that he had better waters in his own country, in which he had often bathed and

never been cleansed of his leprosy; and so remembering this, he did not obey the command of the prophet, yet on the advice and persuasion of his servants he yielded and dipped himself. And being forthwith cleansed, he understood that it is not of the waters but of grace that a man is cleansed. [2846]

18. Understand now who is that young maid among the captives. She is the congregation gathered out of the Gentiles, that is, the Church of God held down of old by the captivity of sin, when as yet it possessed not the liberty of grace, by whose counsel that foolish people of the Gentiles heard the word of prophecy as to which it had before been in doubt. Afterwards, however, when they believed that it ought to be obeyed, they were washed from every defilement of sin. And he indeed doubted before he was healed; you are already healed, and therefore ought not to doubt.

[2834] 1 Cor. v. 18.

[2835] Rom. i. 20.

[2836] S. John x. 38.

[2837] Gen. i. 2.

[2838] Ps. xxxiii. [xxxii.] 6.

[2839] Gen. vi. 3.

[2840] Gen. vii. 1 ff.

[2841] 1 Cor. x. 1, 2.

[2842] Ex. xv. 10.

[2843] S. Luke i. 35.

[2844] S. John i. 17.

[2845] Ex. xv. 23 ff.

[2846] 2 [4] Kings v. 1 ff.

Chapter IV.
That water does not cleanse without the Spirit is shown by the witness of John and by the very form of the administration of the sacrament. And this is also declared to be signified by the pool in the Gospel and the man who was there healed. In the same passage, too, is shown that the Holy Spirit truly descended on Christ at His baptism, and the meaning of this mystery is explained.

19. The reason why you were told before not to believe only what you saw was that you might not say perchance, This is that great mystery "which eye hath not seen, nor ear heard, neither has it entered into the heart of man." [2847] I see water, which I have been used to see every day. Is that water to cleanse me now in which I have so often bathed without ever being cleansed? By this you may recognize that water does not cleanse without the Spirit.

20. Therefore read that the three witnesses in baptism, the water, the blood, and the Spirit, [2848] are one, for if you take away one of these, the Sacrament of Baptism does not exist. For what is water without the cross of Christ? A common element, without any sacramental effect. Nor, again, is there the Sacrament of Regeneration without water: "For except a man be born again of water and of the Spirit, he cannot enter into the kingdom of God." [2849] Now, even the catechumen believes in the cross of the Lord Jesus, wherewith he too is signed; but unless he be baptized in the Name of the Father,

and of the Son, and of the Holy Spirit, he cannot receive remission of sins nor gain the gift of spiritual grace.

21. So that Syrian dipped himself seven times [2850] under the law, but you were baptized in the Name of the Trinity, you confessed the Father. Call to mind what you did: you confessed the Son, you confessed the Holy Spirit. Mark well the order of things in this faith: you died to the world, and rose again to God. And as though buried to the world in that element, being dead to sin, you rose again to eternal life. Believe, therefore, that these waters are not void of power.

22. Therefore it is said: "An angel of the Lord went down according to the season into the pool, and the water was troubled; and he who first after the troubling of the water went down into the pool was healed of whatsoever disease he was holden." [2851] This pool was at Jerusalem, in which one was healed every year, but no one was healed before the angel had descended. Because of those who believed not the water was troubled as a sign that the angel had descended. They had a sign, you have faith; for them an angel descended, for you the Holy Spirit; for them the creature was troubled, for you Christ Himself, the Lord of the creature, works.

23. Then one was healed, now all are made whole; or more exactly, the Christian people alone, for in some even the water is deceitful. [2852] The baptism of unbelievers heals not but pollutes. The Jew washes pots and cups, as though things without sense were capable of guilt or grace. But do you wash this living cup of yours, that in it your good works may shine and the glory of your grace be bright. For that pool was as a type, that you might believe that the power of God descends upon this font.

24. Lastly, that paralytic was waiting for a man. And what man save the Lord Jesus, born of the Virgin, at Whose coming no longer the shadow should heal men one by one, but the truth should heal the whole. He it is, then, Whose coming down was being waited for, of Whom the Father said to John the Baptist: "Upon Whom thou shalt see the Spirit descending and abiding upon Him, this is He Who baptizeth with the Holy Spirit." [2853] And John bare witness of Him, and said: "I saw the Spirit descending from heaven like a dove and abiding upon Him." [2854] And why did the Spirit descend like a dove, but in order that you might see, that you might acknowledge, that that dove also which just Noah sent forth from the ark was a likeness of this dove, that you might recognize the type of the sacrament?

25. Perhaps you may object: Since that was a real dove which was sent forth, and the Spirit descended like a dove, how is it that we say that the likeness was there and the reality here, whereas in the Greek it is written that the Spirit descended in the likeness of a dove? But what is so real as the Godhead which abides for ever? Now the creature cannot be the reality, but only a likeness, which is easily destroyed and changed. So, again, because the simplicity of those who are baptized ought to be not in appearance but in reality, and the Lord says: "Be ye wise as serpents and simple as doves." [2855] Rightly, then, did He descend like a dove, in order to admonish us that we ought to have the simplicity of the dove. And further we read of the likeness being put for the reality, both as regards Christ: "And was found in likeness as a man;" [2856] and as regards God the Father: "Nor have ye seen His likeness." [2857]

[2847] 1 Cor. ii. 9.

[2848] 1 John v. 7.

[2849] S. John iii. 5.

[2850] 2 [4] Kings v. 14.

[2851] S. John v. 4.

[2852] Jer. xv. 18.

[2853] S. John i. 33.

[2854] S. John i. 32.

[2855] S. Matt. x. 16.

[2856] Phil. ii. 8.

[2857] S. John v. 37.

Chapter V.
Christ is Himself present in Baptism, so that we need not consider the person of His ministers. A brief explanation of the confession of the Trinity as usually uttered by those about to be baptized.

26. Is there, then, here any room left for doubt, when the Father clearly calls from heaven in the Gospel narrative, and says: "This is My beloved Son, in Whom I am well pleased"? [2858] When the Son also speaks, upon Whom the Holy Spirit showed Himself in the likeness of a dove? When the Holy Spirit also speaks, Who came down in the likeness of a dove? When David, too, speaks: "The voice of the Lord is above the waters, the God of glory thundered, the Lord above many waters"? [2859] When Scripture testifies that at the prayer of Jerubbaal, fire came down from heaven, [2860] and again, when

Elijah prayed, fire was sent forth and consecrated the sacrifice. [2861]

27. Do not consider the merits of individuals, but the office of the priests. Or, if you look at the merits, consider the priest as Elijah. Look upon the merits of Peter also, or of Paul, who handed down to us this mystery which they had received of the Lord Jesus. To those [of old] a visible fire was sent that they might believe; for us who believe, the Lord works invisibly; for them that happened for a figure, for us for warning. Believe, then, that the Lord Jesus is present at the invocation of the priest, Who said: "Where two or three are, there am I also." [2862] How much where the Church is, and where His Mysteries are, does He vouchsafe to impart His presence!

28. You went down, then (into the water), remember what you replied to the questions, that you believe in the Father, that you believe in the Son, that you believe in the Holy Spirit. The statement there is not: I believe in a greater and in a less and in a lowest person, but you are bound by the same guarantee of your own voice, to believe in the Son in like manner as you believe in the Father; and to believe in the Holy Spirit in like manner as you believe in the Son, with this one exception, that you confess that you must believe in the cross of the Lord Jesus alone.

 [2858] S. Matt. iii. 17.

[2859] Ps. xxix. [xxviii.] 3.

[2860] Judg. vi. 21.

[2861] 1 [3] Kings xviii. 38.

[2862] S. Matt. xviii. 20.

Chapter VI.
Why they who come forth from the laver of baptism are anointed on the head; why, too, after baptism, their feet are washed, and what sins are remitted in each case.

29. After this, you went up to the priest, consider what followed. Was it not that of which David speaks: "Like the ointment upon the head, which went down to the beard, even Aaron's beard"? [2863] This is the ointment of which Solomon, too, says: "Thy Name is ointment poured out, therefore have the maidens loved Thee and drawn Thee." [2864] How many souls regenerated this day have loved Thee, Lord Jesus, and have said: "Draw us after Thee, we are running after the odour of Thy garments," [2865] that they might drink in the odour of Thy resurrection.

30. Consider now why this is done, for "the eyes of a wise man are in his head;" [2866] therefore the ointment flows down to the beard, that is to say, to the beauty of youth; and therefore, Aaron's beard, that we, too, may become a chosen race, priestly and precious, for we are all anointed with spiritual grace for a share in the kingdom of God and in the priesthood.

31. You went up from the font; remember the Gospel lesson. For our Lord Jesus Christ in the Gospel washed the feet of His disciples. When He came to Simon Peter, Peter said: "Thou shalt never wash my feet." [2867] He did not perceive the mystery, and therefore he refused the service, for he thought that the humility of the servant would be injured, if he patiently allowed the Lord to minister to him. And the Lord answered him: "If I wash not thy feet, thou wilt have no part with Me." Peter, hearing this, replies: "Lord, not my feet only, but also my hands and my head." The Lord answered: "He that is washed

needeth not save to wash his feet but is clean every whit."
[2868]

32. Peter was clean, but he must wash his feet, for he had sin by succession from the first man, when the serpent overthrew him and persuaded him to sin. His feet were therefore washed, that hereditary sins might be done away, for our own sins are remitted through baptism.

33. Observe at the same time that the mystery consists in the very office of humility, for Christ says: "If I, your Lord and Master, have washed your feet; how much more ought you to wash one another's feet." For, since the Author of Salvation Himself redeemed us through His obedience, how much more ought we His servants to offer the service of our humility and obedience.

 [2863] Ps. cxxxiii. [cxxxii.] 2.

[2864] Cant. i. 2.

[2865] Cant. i. 3.

[2866] Eccles. ii. 14.

[2867] S. John xiii. 8.

[2868] S. John xiii. 9, 10.

Chapter VII.
The washing away of sins is indicated by the white robes of the catechumens, whence the Church speaks of herself as black and comely. Angels marvel at her brightness as at that of the flesh of the Lord. Moreover, Christ Himself commended His beauty to His Spouse under many figures. The mutual affection of the one for the other is described.

34. After this white robes were given to you as a sign that you were putting off the covering of sins, and putting on the chaste veil of innocence, of which the prophet said: "Thou shalt sprinkle me with hyssop and I shall be cleansed, Thou shalt wash me and I shall be made whiter than snow." [2869] For he who is baptized is seen to be purified both according to the Law and according to the Gospel: according to the Law, because Moses sprinkled the blood of the lamb with a bunch of hyssop; [2870] according to the Gospel, because Christ's garments were white as snow, when in the Gospel He showed forth the glory of His Resurrection. He, then, whose guilt is remitted is made whiter than snow. So that God said by Isaiah: "Though your sins be as scarlet, I will make them white as snow." [2871]

35. The Church, having put on these garments through the laver of regeneration, says in the Song of Songs: "I am black and comely, O daughters of Jerusalem." [2872] Black through the frailty of her human condition, comely through the sacrament of faith. And the daughters of Jerusalem beholding these garments say in amazement: "Who is this that cometh up made white?" [2873] She was black, how is she now suddenly made white?

36. The angels, too, were in doubt when Christ arose; the powers of heaven were in doubt when they saw that flesh was

ascending into heaven. Then they said: "Who is this King of glory?" And whilst some said "Lift up your gates, O princes, and be ye lift up, ye everlasting doors, and the King of glory shall come in." [2874] In Isaiah, too, we find that the powers of heaven doubted and said: "Who is this that cometh up from Edom, the redness of His garments is from Bosor, He who is glorious in white apparel?" [2875]

37. But Christ, beholding His Church, for whom He Himself, as you find in the book of the prophet Zechariah, had put on filthy garments, now clothed in white raiment, seeing, that is, a soul pure and washed in the laver of regeneration, says: "Behold, thou art fair, My love, behold thou art fair, thy eyes are like a dove's," [2876] in the likeness of which the Holy Spirit descended from heaven. The eyes are beautiful like those of a dove, because in the likeness of a dove the Holy Spirit descended from heaven.

38. And farther on: "Thy teeth are like a flock of sheep that are shorn, which are come up from the pool, which all bear twins, and none is barren among them, thy lips are as a cord of scarlet." [2877] This is no slight praise. First by the pleasing comparison to those that are shorn; for we know that goats both feed in high places without risk, and securely find their food in rugged places, and then when shorn are freed from what is superfluous. The Church is likened to a flock of these, having in itself the many virtues of those souls which through the laver lay aside the superfluity of sins, and offer to Christ the mystic faith and the grace of good living, which speak of the cross of the Lord Jesus.

39. The Church is beautiful in them. So that God the Word says to her: "Thou art all fair, My love, and there is no blemish

in thee," for guilt has been washed away. "Come hither from Lebanon, My spouse, come hither from Lebanon, from the beginning of faith wilt thou pass through and pass on," [2878] because, renouncing the world, she passed through things temporal and passed on to Christ. And again, God the Word says to her: "How beautiful and sweet art thou made, O love, in thy delights! Thy stature is become like that of a palm-tree, and thy breasts like bunches of grapes." [2879]

40. And the Church answers Him, "Who will give Thee to me, my Brother, that didst suck the breasts of my mother? If I find Thee without, I will kiss Thee, and indeed they will not despise me. I will take Thee, and bring Thee into the house of my mother; and into the secret chamber of her that conceived me. Thou shalt teach me." [2880] You see how, delighted with the gifts of grace, she longs to attain to the innermost mysteries, and to consecrate all her affections to Christ. She still seeks, she still stirs up His love, and asks of the daughters of Jerusalem to stir it up for her, and desires that by their beauty, which is that of faithful souls, her spouse may be incited to ever richer love for her.

41. So that the Lord Jesus Himself, invited by such eager love and by the beauty of comeliness and grace, since now no offences pollute the baptized, says to the Church: "Place Me as a seal upon thy heart, as a signet upon thine arm;" [2881] that is, thou art comely, My beloved, thou art all fair, nothing is wanting to thee. Place Me as a seal upon thine heart, that thy faith may shine forth in the fulness of the sacrament. Let thy works also shine and set forth the image of God in the Whose image thou wast made. Let no persecution lessen thy love, which many waters cannot quench, nor many rivers drown.

42. And then remember that you received the seal of the Spirit; the spirit of wisdom and understanding, the spirit of counsel and strength, the spirit of knowledge and godliness, and the spirit of holy fear, [2882] and preserved what you received. God the Father sealed you, Christ the Lord strengthened you, and gave the earnest of the Spirit in your heart, [2883] as you have learned in the lesson from the Apostle. [2884]

[2869] Ps. li. [l.] 9.

[2870] Ex. xii. 22.

[2871] Isa. i. 18.

[2872] Cant. i. 4.

[2873] Cant. viii. 5.

[2874] Ps. xxiv. [xxiii.] 8, 9.

[2875] Isa. lxiii. 1.

[2876] Cant. iv. 1.

[2877] Cant. iv. 2, 3.

[2878] Cant. iv. 7, 8.

[2879] Cant. vii. 6, 7.

[2880] Cant. viii. 1, 2.

[2881] Cant. viii. 6.

[2882] Isa. xi. 2.

[2883] 2 Cor. v. 5.

[2884] This passage evidently refers to confirmation, and to the seven gifts of the Holy Spirit received therein. In the Early Church as in the Eastern Church to the present day, confirmation was administered immediately after baptism.

Chapter VIII.
Of the mystical feast of the altar of the Lord. Lest any should think lightly of it, St. Ambrose shows that it is of higher antiquity than the sacred rites of the Jews, since it was foreshadowed in the sacrifice of Melchisedech, and far better than the manna, as being the Body of Christ.

43. The cleansed people, rich with these adornments, hastens to the altar of Christ, saying: "I will go to the altar of God, to God Who maketh glad my youth;" [2885] for having laid aside the slough of ancient error, renewed with an eagle's youth, it hastens to approach that heavenly feast. It comes, and seeing the holy altar arranged, cries out: "Thou hast prepared a table in my sight." David introduces the people as speaking, where he says: "The Lord feedeth me, and nothing shall be wanting to me, in a place of good pasture hath He placed me. He hath led me forth by the water of refreshment." And later: "For though I walk in the midst of the shadow of death, I will fear no evils, for Thou art with me. Thy rod and Thy staff have comforted me. Thou hast prepared in my sight a table against them that trouble me. Thou hast anointed my head with oil, and Thy inebriating cup, how excellent it is!" [2886]

44. We must now pay attention, lest perchance any one seeing that what is visible (for things which are invisible cannot be seen nor comprehended by human eyes), should say, "God rained down manna and rained down quails upon the Jews," [2887] but for the Church beloved of Him the things which He has prepared are those of which it is said: "That eye hath not

seen, nor ear heard, neither hath it entered into the heart of man, what things God hath prepared for them that love Him." [2888] So, lest any one should say this, we will take great pains to prove that the sacraments of the Church are both more ancient than those of the synagogue, and more excellent than the manna.

45. The lesson of Genesis just read shows that they are more ancient, for the synagogue took its origin from the law of Moses. But Abraham was far earlier, who, after conquering the enemy, and recovering his own nephew, as he was enjoying his victory, was met by Melchisedech, who brought forth those things which Abraham reverently received. It was not Abraham who brought them forth, but Melchisedech, who is introduced without father, without mother, having neither beginning of days, nor ending, but like the Son of God, of Whom Paul says to the Hebrews: "that He remaineth a priest for ever," Who in the Latin version is called King of righteousness and King of peace.

46. Do you recognize Who that is? Can a man be king of righteousness, when himself he can hardly be righteous? Can he be king of peace, when he can hardly be peaceable? He it is Who is without mother according to His Godhead, for He was begotten of God the Father, of one substance with the Father; without a father according to His Incarnation, for He was born of a Virgin; having neither beginning nor end, for He is the beginning and end of all things, the first and the last. The sacrament, then, which you received is the gift not of man but of God, brought forth by Him Who blessed Abraham the father of faith, whose grace and deeds we admire.

47. We have proved the sacraments of the Church to be the more ancient, now recognize that they are superior. In very truth it is a marvellous thing that God rained manna on the fathers, and fed them with daily food from heaven; so that it is said, "So man did eat angels' food." [2889] But yet all those who ate that food died in the wilderness, but that food which you receive, that living Bread which came down from heaven, furnishes the substance of eternal life; and whosoever shall eat of this Bread shall never die, and it is the Body of Christ.

49. Now consider whether the bread of angels be more excellent or the Flesh of Christ, which is indeed the body of life. That manna came from heaven, this is above the heavens; that was of heaven, this is of the Lord of the heavens; that was liable to corruption, if kept a second day, this is far from all corruption, for whosoever shall taste it holily shall not be able to feel corruption. For them water flowed from the rock, for you Blood flowed from Christ; water satisfied them for a time, the Blood satiates you for eternity. The Jew drinks and thirsts again, you after drinking will be beyond the power of thirsting; that was in a shadow, this is in truth.

49. If that which you so wonder at is but shadow, how great must that be whose very shadow you wonder at. See now what happened in the case of the fathers was shadow: "They drank, it is said, of that Rock that followed them, and that Rock was Christ. But with many of them God was not well pleased, for they were overthrown in the wilderness. Now these things were done in a figure concerning us." [2890] You recognize now which are the more excellent, for light is better than shadow, truth than a figure, the Body of its Giver than the manna from heaven.

[2885] Ps. xliii. [xlii.] 4.

[2886] Ps. xxiii. [xxii.] 1-5. After being baptized and confirmed in the baptistery, which was detached from the church, the newly "enlightened" were led in solemn procession into the church to be present at the celebration of the Mysteries, and to receive their first communion.

[2887] Ex. xvi. 13.

[2888] 1 Cor. ii. 9.

[2889] Ps. lxxxviii. [lxxxvii.] 25.

[2890] 1 Cor. x. 4.

Chapter IX.
In order that no one through observing the outward part should waver in faith, many instances are brought forward wherein the outward nature has been changed, and so it is proved that bread is made the true body of Christ. The treatise then is brought to a termination with certain remarks as to the effects of the sacrament, the disposition of the recipients, and such like.

50. Perhaps you will say, "I see something else, how is it that you assert that I receive the Body of Christ?" And this is the point which remains for us to prove. And what evidence shall we make use of? Let us prove that this is not what nature made, but what the blessing consecrated, and the power of blessing is greater than that of nature, because by blessing nature itself is changed.

51. Moses was holding a rod, he cast it down and it became a serpent. [2891] Again, he took hold of the tail of the serpent and it returned to the nature of a rod. You see that by virtue of

the prophetic office there were two changes, of the nature both of the serpent and of the rod. The streams of Egypt were running with a pure flow of water; of a sudden from the veins of the sources blood began to burst forth, and none could drink of the river. Again, at the prophet's prayer the blood ceased, and the nature of water returned. [2892] The people of the Hebrews were shut in on every side, hemmed in on the one hand by the Egyptians, on the other by the sea; Moses lifted up his rod, the water divided and hardened like walls, and a way for the feet appeared between the waves. [2893] Jordan being turned back, returned, contrary to nature, to the source of its stream. [2894] Is it not clear that the nature of the waves of the sea and of the river stream was changed? The people of the fathers thirsted, Moses touched the rock, and water flowed out of the rock. [2895] Did not grace work a result contrary to nature, so that the rock poured forth water, which by nature it did not contain? Marah was a most bitter stream, so that the thirsting people could not drink. Moses cast wood into the water, and the water lost its bitterness, which grace of a sudden tempered. [2896] In the time of Elisha the prophet one of the sons of the prophets lost the head from his axe, which sank. He who had lost the iron asked Elisha, who cast in a piece of wood and the iron swam. This, too, we clearly recognize as having happened contrary to nature, for iron is of heavier nature than water.

52. We observe, then, that grace has more power than nature, and yet so far we have only spoken of the grace of a prophet's blessing. But if the blessing of man had such power as to change nature, what are we to say of that divine consecration where the very words of the Lord and Saviour operate? For that sacrament which you receive is made what it is by the word

of Christ. But if the word of Elijah had such power as to bring down fire from heaven, shall not the word of Christ have power to change the nature of the elements? You read concerning the making of the whole world: "He spake and they were made, He commanded and they were created." [2897] Shall not the word of Christ, which was able to make out of nothing that which was not, be able to change things which already are into what they were not? For it is not less to give a new nature to things than to change them.

53. But why make use of arguments? Let us use the examples He gives, and by the example of the Incarnation prove the truth of the mystery. Did the course of nature proceed as usual when the Lord Jesus was born of Mary? If we look to the usual course, a woman ordinarily conceives after connection with a man. And this body which we make is that which was born of the Virgin. Why do you seek the order of nature in the Body of Christ, seeing that the Lord Jesus Himself was born of a Virgin, not according to nature? It is the true Flesh of Christ which crucified and buried, this is then truly the Sacrament of His Body.

54. The Lord Jesus Himself proclaims: "This is My Body." [2898] Before the blessing of the heavenly words another nature is spoken of, after the consecration the Body is signified. He Himself speaks of His Blood. Before the consecration it has another name, after it is called Blood. And you say, Amen, that is, It is true. Let the heart within confess what the mouth utters, let the soul feel what the voice speaks.

55. Christ, then, feeds His Church with these sacraments, by means of which the substance of the soul is strengthened, and seeing the continual progress of her grace, He rightly says to

her: "How comely are thy breasts, my sister, my spouse, how comely they are made by wine, and the smell of thy garments is above all spices. A dropping honeycomb are thy lips, my spouse, honey and milk are under thy tongue, and the smell of thy garments is as the smell of Lebanon. A garden enclosed is my sister, my spouse, a garden enclosed, a fountain sealed." [2899] By which He signifies that the mystery ought to remain sealed up with you, that it be not violated by the deeds of an evil life, and pollution of chastity, that it be not made known to thou, for whom it is not fitting, nor by garrulous talkativeness it be spread abroad amongst unbelievers. Your guardianship of the faith ought therefore to be good, that integrity of life and silence may endure unblemished.

56. For which reason, too, the Church, guarding the depth of the heavenly mysteries, repels the furious storms of wind, and calls to her the sweetness of the grace of spring, and knowing that her garden cannot displease Christ, invites the Bridegroom, saying: "Arise, O north wind, and come, thou south; blow upon my garden, and let my ointments flow down. Let my Brother come down to His garden, and eat the fruit of His trees." [2900] For it has good trees and fruitful, which have dipped their roots in the water of the sacred spring, and with fresh growth have shot forth into good fruits, so as now not to be cut with the axe of the prophet, but to abound with the fruitfulness of the Gospel.

57. Lastly, the Lord also, delighted with their fertility, answers: "I have entered into My garden, My sister, My spouse; I have gathered My myrrh with My spices, I have eaten My meat with My honey, I have drunk My drink with My milk." [2901] Understand, you faithful, why He spoke of meat and drink. And there is no doubt that He Himself eats and drinks in us, as

you have read that He says that in our persons He is in prison. [2902]

58. Wherefore, too, the Church, beholding so great grace, exhorts her sons and her friends to come together to the sacraments, saying: "Eat, my friends, and drink and be inebriated, my brother." [2903] What we eat and what we drink the Holy Spirit has elsewhere made plain by the prophet, saying, "Taste and see that the Lord is good, blessed is the man that hopeth in Him." [2904] In that sacrament is Christ, because it is the Body of Christ, it is therefore not bodily food but spiritual. Whence the Apostle says of its type: "Our fathers ate spiritual food and drank spiritual drink," [2905] for the Body of God is a spiritual body; the Body of Christ is the Body of the Divine Spirit, for the Spirit is Christ, as we read: "The Spirit before our face is Christ the Lord." [2906] And in the Epistle of Peter we read: "Christ died for us." [2907] Lastly, that food strengthens our heart, and that drink "maketh glad the heart of man," [2908] as the prophet has recorded.

59. So, then, having obtained everything, let us know that we are born again, but let us not say, How are we born again? Have we entered a second time into our mother's womb and been born again? I do not recognize here the course of nature. But here there is no order of nature, where is the excellence of grace. And again, it is not always the course of nature which brings about conception, for we confess that Christ the Lord was conceived of a Virgin, and reject the order of nature. For Mary conceived not of man, but was with child of the Holy Spirit, as Matthew says: "She was found with child of the Holy Spirit." [2909] If, then, the Holy Spirit coming down upon the Virgin wrought the conception, and effected the work of generation, surely we must not doubt but that, coming down

upon the Font, or upon those who receive Baptism, He effects the reality of the new birth.

[2891] Ex. iv. 3, 4.

[2892] Ex. vii. 20 ff.

[2893] Ex. xiv. 21 ff.

[2894] Josh. iii. 16.

[2895] Ex. xvii. 6.

[2896] Ex. xv. 25.

[2897] Ps. iii. 5.

[2898] S. Matt. xxvi. 26.

[2899] Cant. iv. 10 ff.

[2900] Cant. iv. 15; v. 1.

[2901] Cant. v. 1.

[2902] S. Matt. xxv. 36.

[2903] Cant. v. 1.

[2904] Ps. xxxiv. [xxxiii.] 9.

[2905] 1 Cor. x. 3.

[2906] Lam. iv. 20.

[2907] 1 Pet. ii. 21.

[2908] Ps. civ. [ciii.] 15.

[2909] S. Matt. i. 18.

Two Books Concerning Repentance.

Introduction.

These two books were written against the Novatian heresy, which took its name, and to a considerable extent its form, from Novatus, a priest of the Church of Carthage, and Novatian, schismatically consecrated bishop at Rome. It was the outcome of a struggle which had long existed in the Church upon the question of the restitution to Church privileges of those who had fallen into grievous sin, and the possibility of their repentance.

The severest ground was taken by the Novatians, who were condemned successively by many councils, which maintained the power of the Church to admit those guilty of any sin whatsoever to repentance, and prescribed various rules and penalties applicable to different cases. The heresy, however, lasted for some time, becoming weaker in the fifth century, and gradually fading away as a separate body with a distinctive name. "Novatianism, in the tests which it used, its efforts after a perfectly pure communion, its crotchetty interpretations of Scripture, and many other features, presents a striking parallel to many modern sects." [See Dict. Chr. Biog., Blunt, Sects and heresies, Ceillier, II. 427, etc.]

St. Ambrose, in writing against the Novatians, seems to have had some recent publication of theirs in his mind, which is now unknown. He begins by commending gentleness, a quality singularly wanting in the sect; speaks of the power committed to the Church of forgiving the greatest sins, and points out how God is more inclined to mercy than to severity, and refutes the arguments of the Novatians based on certain passages of holy Scripture. In the second book, after urging the necessity of careful and speedy repentance, and the necessity of confessing one's sins, St. Ambrose meets the Novatian arguments based on Heb. vi. 4-6, from which they inferred the impossibility of restoration; and on St. Matt. xii. 31, 32, our Lord's words concerning sin against the Holy Spirit.

As regards the date of this treatise, it must have been somewhat before the exposition of Ps. xxxvii., which refers to it, but there is nothing else which can be taken as a certain guide. Possibly the Benedictine Editors are right in assigning it to about a.d. 384.

Some few persons, probably on doctrinal grounds, have been led to question the authorship of this treatise, but it is quoted by St. Augustine, and there has never been any real doubt on the subject.

Book I.

Chapter I.
St. Ambrose writes in praise of gentleness, pointing out how needful that grace is for the rulers of the Church, and commended to them by the meekness of Christ. As the Novatians have fallen away from this, they cannot be considered disciples of Christ. Their pride and harshness are inveighed against.

1. If the highest end of virtue is that which aims at the advancement of most, gentleness is the most lovely of all, which does not hurt even those whom it condemns, and usually renders those whom it condemns worthy of absolution. Moreover, it is the only virtue which has led to the increase of the Church which the Lord sought at the price of His own Blood, imitating the lovingkindness of heaven, and aiming at the redemption of all, seeks this end with a gentleness which the ears of men can endure, in presence of which their hearts do not sink, nor their spirits quail.

2. For he who endeavours to amend the faults of human weakness ought to bear this very weakness on his own shoulders, let it weigh upon himself, not cast it off. For we read that the Shepherd in the Gospel [2910] carried the weary sheep, and did not cast it off. And Solomon says: "Be not overmuch righteous;" [2911] for restraint should temper righteousness. For how shall he offer himself to you for healing whom you despise, who thinks that he will be an object of contempt, not of compassion, to his physician?

3. Therefore had the Lord Jesus compassion upon us in order to call us to Himself, not frighten us away. He came in meekness, He came in humility, and so He said: "Come unto

Me, all ye that labour and are heavy laden, and I will refresh you." [2912] So, then, the Lord Jesus refreshes, and does not shut out nor cast off, and fitly chose such disciples as should be interpreters of the Lord's will, as should gather together and not drive away the people of God. Whence it is clear that they are not to be counted amongst the disciples of Christ, who think that harsh and proud opinions should be followed rather than such as are gentle and meek; persons who, while they themselves seek God's mercy, deny it to others, such as are the teachers of the Novatians, who call themselves pure. [2913]

4. What can show more pride than this, since the Scripture says: "No one is free from sin, not even an infant of a day old;" [2914] and David cries out: "Cleanse me from my sin." [2915] Are they more holy than David, of whose family Christ vouchsafed to be born in the mystery of the Incarnation, whose descendant is that heavenly Hall which received the world's Redeemer in her virgin womb? For what is more harsh than to inflict a penance which they do not relax, and by refusing pardon to take away the incentive to penance and repentance? [2916] Now no one can repent to good purpose unless he hopes for mercy.

[2910] S. Luke xv. 5.

[2911] Eccles. vii. 17.

[2912] S. Matt. xi. 28.

[2913] In order to distinguish themselves from Catholics the Novatians assumed the name katharoi "pure."

[2914] Job xiv. 4 [LXX loosely].

[2915] Ps. li. [l.] 2.

[2916] It is necessary to vary the translation of the word poenitentia in this place, as it bears the meaning both of "penance," the temporal punishment inflicted on the sinner, and also of "repentance."

Chapter II.
The assertion of the Novatians that they refuse communion only to the lapsed agrees neither with the teaching of holy Scripture nor with their own. And whereas they allege as a pretext their reverence for the divine power, they really are contemning it, inasmuch as it is a sign of low estimation not to use the whole of a power entrusted to one. But the Church rightly claims the power of binding and loosing, which heretics have not, inasmuch as she has received it from the Holy Spirit, against Whom they act presumptuously.

5. But they say that those should not be restored to communion who have fallen into denial [2917] of the faith. If they made the crime of sacrilege the only exception to receiving forgiveness, they would be acting harshly indeed, and, as it would seem, would be in opposition to the divine utterances only, while consistent with their own assertions. For when the Lord forgave all sins, He made an exception of none. But since, as it were after the fashion of the Stoics, they think that all sins are equal in gravity, and assert that he who has stolen a common fowl, as they say, no less than he who has smothered his father, should be for ever excluded from the divine mysteries, how can they select those guilty of one special offence, since even they themselves cannot deny that it is most unjust that the penalty of one should extend to many? [2918]

6. They affirm that they are showing great reverence for God, to Whom alone they reserve the power of forgiving sins. But in truth none do Him greater injury than they who choose to

prune His commandments and reject the office entrusted to them. For inasmuch as the Lord Jesus Himself said in the Gospel: "Receive ye the Holy Spirit: whosoever sins ye forgive they are forgiven unto them, and whosoever sins ye retain, they are retained," [2919] who is it that honours Him most, he who obeys His bidding or he who rejects it?

7. The Church holds fast its obedience on either side, by both retaining and remitting sin; heresy is on the one side cruel, and on the other disobedient; wishes to bind what it will not loosen, and will not loosen what it has bound, whereby it condemns itself by its own sentence. For the Lord willed that the power of binding and of loosing should be alike, and sanctioned each by a similar condition. So he who has not the power to loose has not the power to bind. For as, according to the Lord's word, he who has the power to bind has also the power to loose, their teaching destroys itself, inasmuch as they who deny that they have the power of loosing ought also to deny that of binding. For how can the one be allowed and the other disallowed? It is plain and evident that either each is allowed or each is disallowed in the case of those to whom each has been given. Each is allowed to the Church, neither to heresy, for this power has been entrusted to priests alone. Rightly, therefore, does the Church claim it, which has true priests; heresy, which has not the priests of God, [2920] cannot claim it. And by not claiming this power heresy pronounces its own sentence, that not possessing priests it cannot claim priestly power. And so in their shameless obstinacy a shamefaced acknowledgment meets our view.

8. Consider, too, the point that he who has received the Holy Ghost has also received the power of forgiving and of retaining sin. For thus it is written: "Receive the Holy Spirit:

whosesoever sins ye forgive, they are forgiven unto them, and whosesoever sins ye retain, they are retained." [2921] So, then, he who has not received power to forgive sins has not received the Holy Spirit. The office of the priest is a gift of the Holy Spirit, and His right it is specially to forgive and to retain sins. How, then, can they claim His gift who distrust His power and His right?

9. And what is to be said of their excessive arrogance? For although the Spirit of God is more inclined to mercy than to severity, their will is opposed to that which He wills, and they do that which He wills not; whereas it is the office of a judge to punish, but of mercy to forgive. It would be more endurable, Novatian, that thou shouldst forgive than that thou shouldst bind. In the one case thou wouldst assume the right as one who rarely offended; in the other thou wouldst forgive as one who had fellow-feeling with the misery of sin.

[2917] Praevaricatio.

[2918] i.e. the penalty of the one sin of denying the faith should be extended to all sins.

[2919] S. John xx. 22, 23.

[2920] This is not a denial of the validity of Novatian ordinations, which were admitted by the 8th Canon of the Council of Nicaea, but of their lawful jurisdiction.

[2921] S. John xx. 22, 23.

Chapter III.
To the argument of the Novatians, that they only deny forgiveness in the case of greater sins, St. Ambrose replies, that this is also an offence against God, Who gave the power to

forgive all sins, but that of course a more severe penance must follow in case of graver sins. He points out likewise that this distinction as to the gravity of sins assigns, as it were, severity to God, Whose mercy in the Incarnation is overlooked by the Novatians.

10. But they say that, with the exception of graver sins, they grant forgiveness to those of less weight. This is not the teaching of your father, Novatian, who thought that no one should be admitted to penance, considering that what he was unable to loose he would not bind, [2922] lest by binding he should inspire the hope that he would loose. So that your father is condemned by your own sentence, you who make a distinction between sins, some of which you consider that you can loose, and others which you consider to be without remedy. But God does not make a distinction, Who has promised His mercy to all, and granted to His priests the power of loosing without any exception. But he who has heaped up sin must also increase his penitence. For greater sins are washed away by greater weeping. So neither is Novatian justified, who excluded all from pardon; nor are you, who imitate and, at the same time, condemn him, for you diminish zeal for penance where it ought to be increased, since the mercy of Christ has taught us that graver sins must be made good by greater efforts.

11. And what perversity it is to claim for yourselves what can be forgiven, and, as you say, to reserve to God what cannot be forgiven. This would be to reserve to oneself the cases for mercy, to God those for severity. And what as to that saying: "Let God be true but every man a liar, as it is written, That Thou mightest be justified in Thy words, and overcome when Thou art judged"? [2923] In order, then, that we may recognize that the God of mercy is rather prone to indulgence than to

severity, it is said: "I desire mercy rather than sacrifice." [2924] How, then, can your sacrifice, who refuse mercy, be acceptable to God, since He says that He wills not the death of a sinner, but his correction? [2925]

12. Interpreting which truth, the Apostle says: "For God, sending His own Son in the likeness of sinful flesh, and for sin condemned sin in the flesh, that the righteousness of the Law might be fulfilled in us." [2926] He does not say "in the likeness of flesh," for Christ took on Himself the reality not the likeness of flesh; nor does He say in the likeness of sin, for He did no sin, but was made sin for us. Yet He came "in the likeness of sinful flesh;" that is, He took on Him the likeness of sinful flesh, the likeness, because it is written: "He is man, and who shall know Him?" [2927] He was man in the flesh, according to His human nature, that He might be recognized, but in power was above man, that He might not be recognized, so He has our flesh, but has not the failings of this flesh.

13. For He was not begotten, as is every man, by intercourse between male and female, but born of the Holy Spirit and of the Virgin; He received a stainless body, which not only no sins polluted, but which neither the generation nor the conception had been stained by any admixture of defilement. For we men are all born under sin, and our very origin is in evil, as we read in the words of David: "For lo, I was conceived in wickedness, and in sin did my mother bring me forth." [2928] Therefore the flesh of Paul was a body of death, as he himself says: "Who shall deliver me from the body of this death?" [2929] But the flesh of Christ condemned sin, which He felt not at His birth, and crucified by His death, so that in our flesh there might be justification through grace, in which before there had been pollution by guilt.

14. What, then, shall we say to this, except that which the Apostle said: "If God is for us, who is against us? He who spared not His own Son, but gave Him up for us all, how has He not with Him also given us all things? Who shall lay a charge against the elect? It is God Who justifieth, who is he that shall condemn? It is Christ Who died, yea, Who also rose again, Who is at the right hand of God, Who also maketh intercession for us." [2930] Novatian then brings charges against those for whom Christ intercedes. Those whom Christ has redeemed unto salvation Novatian condemns to death. Those to whom Christ says: "Take My yoke upon you, and learn of Me, for I am gentle," [2931] Novatian says, I am not gentle. On those to whom Christ says: "Ye shall find rest for your souls, for My yoke is pleasant and My burden is light," [2932] Novatian lays a heavy burden and a hard yoke.

[2922] Binding and loosing here refer rather to the infliction of open penance, the outward sign of repentance, than to absolution.

[2923] Rom. iii. 4.

[2924] Hosea vi. 6.

[2925] Ezek. xviii. 32.

[2926] Rom. viii. 3, 4.

[2927] Jerem. xvii. 9 [LXX.].

[2928] Ps. li. [l.] 5.

[2929] Rom. vii. 24.

[2930] Rom. viii. 31-35.

[2931] S. Matt. xi. 29.

[2932] S. Matt. xi. 30.

Chapter IV.
St. Ambrose proceeds with the proof of the divine mercy, and shows by the testimony of the Gospels that it prevails over severity, and he adduces the instance of athletes to show that of those who have denied Christ before men, all are not to be esteemed alike.

15. Although what has been said sufficiently shows how inclined the Lord Jesus is to mercy, let Him further instruct us with His own words, when He would arm us against the assaults of persecution. "Fear not," He says, "those who kill the body, but cannot kill the soul, but rather fear Him Who can cast both body and soul into hell." [2933] And farther on: "Every one, therefore, who shall confess Me before men, him will I also confess before My Father, Who is in heaven, but he who shall deny Me before men, him will I also deny before My Father, Who is in heaven." [2934]

16. Where He says that He will confess, He will confess "every one." [2935] Where He speaks of denying, He does not speak of denying "every one." For, whereas in the former clause He says, "Every one who shall confess Me, him will I confess," we should expect that in the following clause He would also say, "Every one who shall deny Me." But in order that He might not appear to deny every one, He concludes: "But he who shall deny Me before men, him will I also deny." He promises favour to every one, but He does not threaten the penalty to every one. He makes more of that which is merciful. He makes less of what is penal.

17. And this is written not only in that book of the Gospel of the Lord Jesus, which is written according to Matthew, but it is also to be read in that which we have according to Luke, [2936] that we might know that neither had thus related the saying by chance.

18. We have said that it is thus written. Let us now consider the meaning. "Every one," He says, "who shall confess Me," that is to say, of whatever age, of whatever condition he may be, who shall confess Me, he shall have Me as the Rewarder of his confession. Whereas the expression is, "every one," no one who shall confess is excluded from the reward. But it is not said in like manner, "Every one who shall deny shall be denied," for it is possible that a man overcome by torture may deny God in word, and yet worship Him in his heart.

19. Is the case the same with him who denies voluntarily, and with him whom torture, not his own will, has led to denial? How unfit were it, since with men credit is given for endurance in a struggle, that one should assert that it had no value with God! For often in this world's athletic contests the public crown together with the victors even the vanquished whose conduct has been approved, especially if perchance they have seen that they lost the victory by some trick or fraud. And shall Christ suffer His athletes, whom He has seen to yield for a moment to severe torments, to remain without forgiveness?

20. Shall not He take account of their toil, Who will not cast off for ever even those whom He casts off? For David says: "God will not cast off for ever," [2937] and in opposition to this shall we listen to heresy asserting, "He does cast off for ever"? David says: "God will not for ever cut off His mercy from generation to generation, nor will He forget to be merciful." [2938] This is

the prophet's declaration, and there are those who would maintain a forgetfulness of mercy on God's part.

[2933] S. Matt. x. 28.

[2934] S. Matt. x. 32, 33.

[2935] Omnis.

[2936] S. Luke xii. 8, 9.

[2937] Ps. lxxvii. [lxxvi.] 7. In the Psalm this passage is a question of the Psalmist in his bitter troubles, "Will God cast off?" St. Ambrose, in arguing against Novatian, not only modifies the text, but somewhat modifies its meaning.

[2938] Ps. lxxvii. [lxxvi.] 8, 9.

Chapter V.
The objection from the unchangeableness of God is answered from several passages of Scripture, wherein God promises forgiveness to sinners on their repentance. St. Ambrose also shows that mercy will be more readily accorded to such as have sinned, as it were, against their will, which he illustrates by the case of prisoners taken in war, and by language put into the mouth of the devil.

21. But they say that they make these assertions in order not to seem to make God liable to change, as He would be if He forgave those with whom He was angry. What then? Shall we reject the utterances of God and follow their opinions? But God is not to be judged by the statements of others, but by His own words. What mark of His mercy have we more ready at hand than that He Himself, through the prophet Hosea, is at once merciful as though reconciled to those whom in His anger He had threatened? For He says: "O Ephraim, what shall I do

unto thee, or what shall I do unto thee, O Judah? Your kindness," etc. [2939] And further on: "How shall I establish thee? I will make thee as Admah, and as Zeboim." [2940] In the midst of His indignation He hesitates, as it were, with fatherly love, doubting how He can give over the wanderer to punishment; for although the Jew deserves it, God yet takes counsel with Himself. For immediately after having said, "I will make thee as Admah and as Zeboim," which cities, owing to their nearness to Sodom, suffered together in like destruction, He adds, "My heart is turned against Me, My compassion is aroused, I will not do according to the fierceness of Mine anger." [2941]

22. Is it not evident that the Lord Jesus is angry with us when we sin in order that He may convert us through fear of His indignation? His indignation, then, is not the carrying out of vengeance, but rather the working out of forgiveness, for these are His words: "If thou shalt turn and lament, thou shalt be saved." [2942] He waits for our lamentations here, that is, in time, that He may spare us those which shall be eternal. He waits for our tears, that He may pour forth His goodness. So in the Gospel, having pity on the tears of the widow, He raised her son. He waits for our conversion, that He may Himself restore us to grace, which would have continued with us had no fall overtaken us. But He is angry because we have by our sins incurred guilt, in order that we may be humbled; we are humbled, in order that we may be found worthy rather of pity than of punishment.

23. Jeremiah, too, may certainly teach when he says: "For the Lord will not cast off for ever; for after He has humbled, He will have compassion according to the multitude of His mercies, Who hath not humbled from His whole heart nor cast

off the children of men." [2943] This passage we certainly find in the Lamentations of Jeremiah, and from it, and from what follows, we note that the Lord humbles all the prisoners of the earth under His feet, [2944] in order that we may escape His judgment. But He does not bring down the sinner even to the earth with His whole heart Who raises the poor even from the dust and the needy from the dunghill. For He brings not down with His whole heart Who reserves the intention of forgiving.

24. But if He brings not down every sinner with His whole heart, how much less does He bring down him with His whole heart who has not sinned with his whole heart! For as He said of the Jews: "This people honoureth Me with their lips, but their heart is far from Me," [2945] so perhaps He may say of some of the fallen: "They denied Me with their lips, but in heart they are with Me. It was pain which overcame them, not unfaithfulness which turned them aside." [2946] But some without cause refuse pardon to those whose faith the persecutor himself confessed up to the point of striving to overcome it by torture. They denied the Lord once, but confess Him daily; they denied Him in word, but confess Him with groans, with cries, and with tears; they confess Him with willing words, not under compulsion. They yielded, indeed, for a moment to the temptation of the devil, but even the devil afterwards departed from those whom he was unable to claim as his own. He yielded to their weeping, he yielded to their repentance, and after making them his own lost those whom he attached when they belonged to Another.

25. Is not the case such as when any one carries away captive the people of a conquered city? The captive is led away, but against his will. He must of necessity go to foreign lands, does not willingly make the journey; he takes his native land with

him in his heart, and seeks an opportunity to return. What then? When any such return, does any one urge that they should not be received; with less honour indeed, but with readier will, that the enemy may have nothing with which to reproach them? If you pardon an armed man who was able to fight, do you not pardon him in whom faith alone waged the battle?

26. If we were to enquire what is the opinion of the devil concerning those who have fallen after this sort, would he not probably reply: "This people honours me with their lips, but their heart is far from me? For how can he be with me who does not depart from Christ? Without any cause do they appear to honour me who keep the doctrine of Jesus, and I thought that they would teach mine. They condemn me all the more when they forsake me after trial. Indeed Jesus is more glorified in these, when He receives them on their return to Him. All the angels rejoice, for in heaven there is greater joy over one sinner that repents, than over ninety and nine just persons who need not repentance. I am triumphed over in heaven and on earth. Christ loses nothing when they who came to me with weeping return with longing to the Church, and I am in danger even as regards my own, who will learn that in reality there is nothing here where men are led on by present rewards, but that there must be very much there where groans and tears and fasts are preferred to my feasts."

[2939] Hos. vi. 4.

[2940] Hos. xi. 8.

[2941] Hos. xi. 8.

[2942] Ps. xxx. 15 [LXX.].

[2943] Lam. iii. 31, 32.

[2944] Lam. iii. 34.

[2945] Isa. xxix. 13.

[2946] S. Matt. xv. 8.

Chapter VI.
The Novatians, by excluding such from the banquet of Christ, imitate not indeed the good Samaritan, but the proud lawyer, the priest, and the Levite who are blamed in the Gospel, and are indeed worse than these.

27. Do you then, O Novatians, shut out these? For what is it when you refuse the hope of forgiveness but to shut out? But the Samaritan did not pass by the man who had been left half dead by the robbers; he dressed his wounds with oil and wine, first pouring in oil in order to comfort them; he set the wounded man on his own beast, on which he bore all his sins; nor did the Shepherd despise His wandering sheep.

28. But you say: "Touch me not." You who wish to justify yourselves say, "He is not our neighbour," being more proud than that lawyer who wished to tempt Christ, for he said "Who is my neighbour?" He asked, you deny, going on like that priest, like that Levite passing by him whom you ought to have taken and tended, and not receiving them into the inn for whom Christ paid the two pence, whose neighbour Christ bids you to become that you might show mercy to him. For he is our neighbour whom not only a similar condition has joined, but whom mercy has bound to us. You make yourself strange to him through pride, in vain puffing up yourself in your carnal mind, and not holding the Head. [2947] For if you held the Head you would consider that you must not forsake him for

whom Christ died. If you held the Head you would consider that the whole body, by joining together rather than by separating, grows unto the increase of God [2948] by the bond of charity and the rescue of a sinner.

29. When, then, you take away all the fruits of repentance, what do you say but this: Let no one who is wounded enter our inn, let no one be healed in our Church? With us the sick are not cared for, we are whole, we have no need of a physician, for He Himself says: "They that are whole need not a physician, but they that are sick."

[2947] Col. ii. 18.

[2948] Col. ii. 19.

Chapter VII.
St. Ambrose, addressing Christ, complains of the Novatians, and shows that they have no part with Christ, Who wishes all men to be saved.

30. So, then, Lord Jesus, come wholly to Thy Church, since Novatian makes excuse. Novatian says, "I have bought a yoke of oxen," and he puts not on the light yoke of Christ, but lays upon his shoulders a heavy burden which he is not able to bear. Novatian held back Thy servants by whom he was invited, treated them contemptuously and slew them, polluting them with the stain of a reiterated baptism. Send forth, therefore, into the highways, and gather together good and bad, [2949] bring the weak, the blind, and the lame into Thy Church. Command that Thy house be filled, bring in all unto Thy supper, for Thou wilt make him whom Thou shalt call worthy, if he follow Thee. He indeed is rejected who has not the

wedding garment, that is, the vestment of charity, the veil of grace. Send forth I pray Thee to all.

31. Thy Church does not excuse herself from Thy supper, Novatian makes excuse. Thy family says not, "I am whole, I need not the physician," but it says: "Heal me, O Lord, and I shall be healed; save me, and I shall be saved." [2950] The likeness of Thy Church is that woman who went behind and touched the hem of Thy garment, saying within herself: "If I do but touch His garment I shall be whole." [2951] So the Church confesses her wounds, but desires to be healed.

32. And Thou indeed, O Lord, desirest that all should be healed, but all do not wish to be healed. Novatian wishes not, who thinks that he is whole. Thou, O Lord, sayest that Thou art sick, and feelest our infirmity in the least of us, saying: "I was sick and ye visited Me." [2952] Novatian does not visit that least one in whom Thou desirest to be visited. Thou saidst to Peter when he excused himself from having his feet washed by Thee: "If I wash not thy feet, thou wilt have no part with Me." [2953] What fellowship, then, can they have with Thee, who receive not the keys of the kingdom of heaven, saying that they ought not to remit sins?

33. And this confession is indeed rightly made by them, for they have not the succession of Peter, who hold not the chair of Peter, which they rend by wicked schism; and this, too, they do, wickedly denying that sins can be forgiven even in the Church, whereas it was said to Peter: "I will give unto thee the keys of the kingdom of heaven, and whatsoever thou shalt bind on earth shall be bound also in heaven, and whatsoever thou shalt loose on earth shall be loosed also in heaven." [2954] And the vessel of divine election himself said: "If ye have forgiven

anything to any one, I forgive also, for what I have forgiven I have done it for your sakes in the person of Christ." [2955] Why, then, do they read Paul's writings, if they think that he has erred so wickedly as to claim for himself the right of his Lord? But he claimed what he had received, he did not usurp that which was not due to him.

[2949] S. Luke xiv. 21.

[2950] Jerem. xvii. 14.

[2951] S. Matt. ix. 21.

[2952] S. Matt. xxv. 36.

[2953] S. John xiii. 8.

[2954] S. Matt. xvi. 19.

[2955] 2 Cor. ii. 10.

Chapter VIII.
It was the Lord's will to confer great gifts on His disciples. Further, the Novatians confute themselves by the practices of laying on of hands and of baptism, since it is by the same power that sins are remitted in penance and in baptism. Their conduct is then contrasted with that of our Lord.

34. It is the will of the Lord that His disciples should possess great powers; it is His will that the same things which He did when on earth should be done in His Name by His servants. For He said: "Ye shall do greater things than these." [2956] He gave them power to raise the dead. And whereas He could Himself have restored to Saul the use of his sight, He nevertheless sent him to His disciple Ananias, that by his blessing Saul's eyes might be restored, the sight of which he had

lost. [2957] Peter also He bade walk with Himself on the sea, and because he faltered He blamed him for lessening the grace given him by the weakness of his faith. [2958] He Who Himself was the light of the world granted to His disciples to be the light of the world through grace. [2959] And because He purposed to descend from heaven and to ascend thither again, He took up Elijah into heaven to restore him again to earth at the time which should please Him. And being baptized with the Holy Spirit and with fire, He foreshadowed the Sacrament of Baptism at the hands of John. [2960]

35. And in fine He gave all gifts to His disciples, of whom He said: "In My Name they shalt cast out devils; they shall speak with new tongues; they shall take up serpents; and if they shall drink any deadly thing it shall not hurt them; they shall lay hands on the sick, and they shall do well." [2961] So, then, He gave them all things, but there is no power of man exercised in these things, in which the grace of the divine gift operates.

36. Why, then, do you lay on hands, and believe it to be the effect of the blessing, if perchance some sick person recovers? Why do you assume that any can be cleansed by you from the pollution of the devil? Why do you baptize if sins cannot be remitted by man? If baptism is certainly the remission of all sins, what difference does it make whether priests claim that this power is given to them in penance or at the font? In each the mystery is one.

37. But you say that the grace of the mysteries works in the font. What works, then, in penance? Does not the Name of God do the work? What then? Do you, when you choose, claim for yourselves the grace of God, and when you choose reject it? But this is a mark of insolent presumption, not of holy

fear, when those who wish to do penance are despised by you. You cannot, forsooth, endure the tears of the weepers; your eyes cannot bear the coarse clothing, the filth of the squalid; with proud eyes and puffed-up hearts you delicate ones say with angry tones, "Touch me not, for I am pure."

38. The Lord said indeed to Mary Magdalene, "Touch Me not," [2962] but He Who was pure did not say, "because I am pure." Do you, Novatian, dare to call yourself pure, whilst, even if you were pure as regards your acts, you would be made impure by this saying alone? Isaiah says: "O wretched that I am, and pricked to the heart; for that being a man, and having unclean lips, I dwell also in the midst of a people having unclean lips," [2963] and do you say, "I am clean," when, as it is written, not even an infant of a day old is pure? [2964] David says, "And cleanse me from my sin," [2965] whom for his tender heart the grace of God often cleansed; are you pure who are so unrighteous as to have no tenderness, as to see the mote in your brother's eye, but not to consider the beam which is in your own eye? For with God no one who is unjust is pure. And what is more unjust than to desire to have your sins forgiven you, and yet yourself to think that he who entreats you ought not to be forgiven? What is more unjust than to justify yourself in that wherein you condemn another, whilst you yourself are committing worse offences?

39. Then, too, the Lord Jesus when about to consecrate [2966] the forgiveness of our sins replied to John, who said: "I ought to be baptized of Thee, and comest Thou to me? Suffer it now, for thus it becometh us to fulfil all righteousness." [2967] And the Lord indeed came to a sinner, though indeed He had no sin, and desired to be baptized, having no need of cleansing; who, then, can tolerate you, who think there is no need for you

to be cleansed by penance, because you say you are cleansed by grace, as though it were now impossible for you to sin?

 [2956] S. John xiv. 12; S. Matt. x. 8.

[2957] Acts ix. 17.

[2958] S. Matt. xiv. 31.

[2959] S. Matt. v. 14.

[2960] S. Matt. iii. 11.

[2961] S. Mark xvi. 17, 18.

[2962] S. John xx. 17.

[2963] Isa. vi. 5.

[2964] Job xiv. 4 [LXX.].

[2965] Ps. li. [l.] 2.

[2966] Celebraturus.

[2967] S. Matt. iii. 14, 15.

Chapter IX.
By collating similar passages with 1 Sam. iii. 25, St. Ambrose shows that the meaning is not that no one shall intercede, but that the intercessor must be worthy as were Moses and Jeremiah, at whose prayers we read that God spared Israel.

40. But you say, It is written: "If a man sin against the Lord, who shall entreat for him?" [2968] First of all, as I already said before, I might allow you to make that objection if you refused penance to those only who denied the faith. But what difficulty

does that question produce? For it is not written, "No one shall entreat for him;" but, "Who shall entreat?" that is to say, the question is, Who in such a case can entreat? The entreaty is not excluded.

41. Then you have in the fifteenth Psalm: "Lord, who shall dwell in Thy tabernacle, or who shall rest upon Thy holy hill?" [2969] It is not that no one, but that he who is approved shall dwell there, nor does it say that no one shall rest, but he who is chosen shall rest. And that you may know that this is true, it is said not much later in the twenty-fourth Psalm: "Who shall ascend into the hill of the Lord, or who shall stand in His holy place?" [2970] The writer implies, not any ordinary person, or one of the common sort, but only a man of excellent life and of singular merit. And that we may understand that when the question is asked, Who? it does not imply no one, but some special one is meant, after having said "Who shall ascend into the hill of the Lord?" the Psalmist adds: "He that hath clean hands and a pure heart, who hath not lift up his mind unto vanity." [2971] And elsewhere it is said: "Who is wise and he shall understand these things?" [2972] And in the Gospel: "Who is the faithful and wise steward, whom the Lord shall set over His household to give them their measure of wheat in due season?" [2973] And that we may understand that He speaks of such as really exist, the Lord added: "Blessed is that servant, whom his Lord when He cometh shall find so doing." [2974] And I am of opinion that where it is said, "Lord, who is like unto Thee?" [2975] it is not meant that none is like, for the Son is the image of the Father.

42. We must then understand in the same manner, "Who shall entreat for him?" as implying: It must be some one of excellent life who shall entreat for him who has sinned against the Lord.

The greater the sin, the more worthy must be the prayers that are sought. For it was not any one of the common people who prayed for the Jewish people, but Moses, [2976] when forgetful of their covenant they worshipped the head of the calf. Was Moses wrong? Certainly he was not wrong in praying, who both merited and obtained that for which he asked. For what should such love not obtain as that of his when he offered himself for the people and said: "And now, if Thou wilt forgive their sin, forgive; but if not, blot me out of the book of life." [2977] We see that he does not think of himself, like a man full of fancies and scruples, whether he may incur the risk of some offence, as Novatian says he dreads that he might, but rather, thinking of all and forgetful of himself, he was not afraid lest he should offend, so that he might rescue and free the people from danger of offence.

43. Rightly, then, is it said: "Who shall entreat for him?" It implies that it must be such an one as Moses to offer himself for those who sin, or such as Jeremiah, who, though the Lord said to him, "Pray not thou for this people," [2978] and yet he prayed and obtained their forgiveness. For at the intercession of the prophet, and the entreaty of so great a seer, the Lord was moved and said to Jerusalem, which had meanwhile repented for its sins, and had said: "O Almighty Lord God of Israel, the soul in anguish, and the troubled spirit crieth unto Thee, hear, O Lord, and have mercy." [2979] And the Lord bids them lay aside the garments of mourning, and to cease the groanings of repentance, saying: "Put off, O Jerusalem, the garment of thy mourning and affliction. and clothe thyself in beauty, the glory which God hath given thee for ever." [2980]

[2968] 1 Sam. [1 Kings] ii. 25.

[2969] Ps. xv. [xiv.] 1.

[2970] Ps. xxiv. [xxiii.] 3.

[2971] Ps. xxiv. [xxiii.] 4.

[2972] Hos. xiv. 10.

[2973] S. Luke xii. 42.

[2974] S. Luke xii. 43.

[2975] Ps. lxxi. [lxx.] 19.

[2976] Ex. xxxii. 31.

[2977] Ex. xxxii. 32.

[2978] Jer. vii. 16.

[2979] Bar. iii. 1, 2.

[2980] Bar. v. 1.

Chapter X.

St. John did not absolutely forbid that prayer should be made for those who "sin unto death," since he knew that Moses, Jeremiah, and Stephen had so prayed, and he himself implies that forgiveness is not to be denied them.

44. Such intercessors, then, must be sought for after very grievous sins, for if any ordinary persons pray they are not heard.

45. So that point of yours will have no weight, which you take from the Epistle of John, where he says: "He who knows that his brother sinneth a sin not unto death, let him ask, and God

will give him life, because he sinned not unto death. There is a sin unto death: not concerning it do I say, let him ask." [2981] He was not speaking to Moses and Jeremiah, but to the people, who must seek another intercessor for their sins; the people, for whom it is sufficient they entreat God for their lighter faults, and consider that pardon for weightier sins must be reserved for the prayers of the just. For how could John say that graver sins should not be prayed for, when he had read that Moses prayed and obtained his request, where there had been wilful casting off of faith, and knew that Jeremiah also had entreated?

46. How could John say that we should not pray for the sin unto death, who himself in the Apocalypse wrote the message to the angel of the Church of Pergamos? "Thou hast there those that hold the doctrine of Balaam, who taught Balac to put a stumbling-block before the children of Israel, to eat things sacrificed unto idols, and to commit fornication. So hast thou also them that hold the doctrines of the Nicolaitans. Repent likewise, or else I will come to thee quickly." [2982] Do you see that the same God Who requires repentance promises forgiveness? And then He says: "He that hath ears let him hear what the Spirit saith to the churches: To him that overcometh will I give to eat of the hidden manna." [2983]

47. Did not John himself know that Stephen prayed for his persecutors, who had not been able even to listen to the Name of Christ, when he said of those very men by whom he was being stoned: "Lord, lay not this sin to their charge"? [2984] And we see the result of this prayer in the case of the Apostle, for Paul, who kept the garments of those who were stoning Stephen, not long after became an apostle by the grace of God, having before been a persecutor.

[2981] 1 John v. 16.

[2982] Rev. ii. 14, 15, 16.

[2983] Rev. ii. 17.

[2984] Acts vii. 60.

Chapter XI.
The passage quoted from St. John's Epistle is confirmed by another in which salvation is promised to those who believe in Christ, which refutes the Novatians who try to induce the lapsed to believe, although denying them pardon. Furthermore, many who had lapsed have received the grace of martyrdom, whilst the example of the good Samaritan shows that we must not abandon those in whom even the faintest amount of faith is still alive.

48. Since, then, we have spoken of the general Epistle of St. John, let us enquire whether the writings of John in the Gospel agree with your interpretation. For he writes that the Lord said: "God so loved this world, that He gave His only-begotten Son, that every one that believeth on Him should not perish but have everlasting life." [2985] If, then, you wish to reclaim any one of the lapsed, do you exhort him to believe, or not to believe? Undoubtedly you exhort him to believe. But, according to the Lord's words, he who believes shall have everlasting life. How, then, will you forbid to pray for him, who has a claim to everlasting life? since faith is of divine grace, as the Apostle teaches where he speaks of the differences of gifts, for "to another is given faith by the same Spirit." [2986] And the disciples say to the Lord: "Increase our faith." [2987] He then who has faith has life, and he who has life is certainly not shut out from pardon; "that every one," it is said, "that believeth on Him should not perish." Since it is said, Every one, no one is

73

shut out, no one is excepted, for He does not except him who has lapsed, if only afterwards he believes effectually.

49. We find that many have at length recovered themselves after a fall, and have suffered for the Name of God. Can we deny fellowship with the martyrs to these to whom the Lord Jesus has not denied it? Do we dare to say that life is not restored to those to whom Christ has given a crown? As, then, a crown is given to many after they have lapsed, so, too, if they believe, their faith is restored, which faith is the gift of God, as you read: "Because unto you it hath been granted by God not only to believe in Him, but also to suffer in His behalf." [2988] Is it possible that he who has the gift of God should not have His forgiveness?

50. Now it is not a single but a twofold grace that every one who believes should also suffer for the Lord Jesus. He, then, who believes receives his grace, but he receives a second, if his faith be crowned by suffering. For neither was Peter without grace before he suffered, but when he suffered he received a second gift. And many who have not had the grace to suffer for Christ have nevertheless had the grace of believing on Him.

51. Therefore it is said: "That every one that believeth in Him should not perish." Let no one, that is, of whatever condition, after whatever fall, fear that he will perish. For it may come to pass that the good Samaritan of the Gospel may find some one going down from Jerusalem to Jericho, that is, falling back from the martyr's conflict to the pleasures of this life and the comforts of the world; wounded by robbers, that is, by persecutors, and left half dead; that good Samaritan, Who is the Guardian of our souls (for the word Samaritan means

Guardian), [2989] may, I say, not pass by him but tend and heal him. [2990]

52. Perchance He therefore passes him not by, because He sees in him some signs of life, so that there is hope that he may recover. Does it not seem to you that he who has fallen is half alive if faith sustains any breath of life? For he is dead who wholly casts God out of his heart. He, then, who does not wholly cast Him out, but under pressure of torments has denied Him for a time, is half dead. Or if he be dead, why do you bid him repent, seeing he cannot now be healed? If he be half dead, pour in oil and wine, not wine without oil, that may be the comfort and the smart. Place him upon thy beast, give him over to the host, lay out two pence for his cure, be to him a neighbour. But you cannot be a neighbour unless you have compassion on him; for no one can be called a neighbour unless he have healed, not killed, another. But if you wish to be called a neighbour, Christ says to you: "Go and do likewise." [2991]

[2985] S. John iii. 16.

[2986] 1 Cor. xii. 9.

[2987] S. Luke xvii. 5.

[2988] Phil. i. 29.

[2989] The Samaritans took their name from the territory which they inhabited. But they called themselves Hebrew [Shomrim], Guardians, that is, of the Law. This idea is referred to here by St. Ambrose as elsewhere by others of the Fathers.

[2990] S. Luke x. 33 ff.

[2991] S. Luke x. 37.

Chapter XII.

Another passage of St. John is considered. The necessity of keeping the commandments of God may be complied with by those who, having fallen, repent, as well as by those who have not fallen, as is shown in the case of David.

53. Let us consider another similar passage: "He that believeth on the Son hath eternal life, but he that believeth not the Son shall not see life, but the wrath of God abideth on him." [2992] That which abideth has certainly had a commencement, and that from some offence, viz., that first he not believe. When, then, any one believes, the wrath of God departs and life comes. To believe, then, in Christ is to gain life, for "he that believeth in Him is not judged." [2993]

54. But with reference to this passage they allege that he who believes in Christ ought to keep His sayings, and say that it is written in the Lord's own words: "I am come a light into this world, that whosoever believeth in Me may not abide in darkness. And if any man hear My word and keep it, I judge him not." [2994] He judges not, and do you judge? He says, "that whosoever believeth on Me may not abide in darkness," that is, that if he be in darkness he may not remain therein, but may amend his error, correct his fault, and keep My commandments, for I have said, "I will not the death of the wicked, but the correction." [2995] I said above that he that believeth on Me is not judged, and I keep to this: "For I am not come to judge the world, but that the world may be saved through Me." [2996] I pardon willingly, I quickly forgive, "I will have mercy rather than sacrifice," [2997] because by sacrifice the just is rendered more acceptable, by mercy the sinner is redeemed. "I come not to call the righteous but sinners." [2998]

Sacrifice was under the Law, in the Gospel is mercy. "The Law was given by Moses, grace by Me." [2999]

55. And again further on He says: "He that despiseth Me, and receiveth not My words, hath one that judgeth him." [3000] Does he seem to you to have received Christ's words who has not corrected himself? Undoubtedly not. He, then, who corrects himself receives His word, for this is His word, that every one should turn back from sin. So, then, of necessity you must either reject this saying of His, or if you cannot deny it you must accept it.

56. It is also necessary that he who leaves off sinning must keep the commandments of God and renounce his sins. We ought not, then, to interpret this saying of him who has always kept the commandments, for if this had been His meaning He would have added the word always, but by not adding it He shows that He was speaking of him who has kept what he has heard, and what he heard has led him to correct his faults; he has then kept what he has heard.

57. But how hard it is to condemn to penance for life one who even afterwards keeps the commandments of the Lord, let Him teach us Himself Who has not refused forgiveness. Even to those who do not keep His commandments, as you read in the Psalm: "If they profane My statutes and keep not My commandments, I will visit their offences with the rod and their sins with scourges, but My mercy will I not take from them." [3001] So, then, He promises mercy to all.

58. Yet that we may not think that this mercy is without judgment, there is a distinction made between those who have paid continual obedience to God's commandments, and those who at some time, either by error or by compulsion, have

fallen. And that you may not think that it is only our arguments which press you, consider the decision of Christ, Who said: "If the servant knew his Lord's will and did it not, he shall be beaten with many stripes, but if he knew it not, he shall be beaten with few stripes." [3002] Each, then, if he believes, is received, for God "chasteneth every son whom He receiveth," [3003] and him whom He chasteneth He does not give over unto death, for it is written: "The Lord hath chastened me sore, but He hath not given me over unto death." [3004]

[2992] S. John iii. 36.

[2993] S. John iii. 18.

[2994] S. John xii. 47 [not exact].

[2995] Ezek. xxiii. 11.

[2996] S. John iii. 17.

[2997] Hosea vi. 6.

[2998] S. Matt. ix. 13.

[2999] S. John i. 17.

[3000] S. John xii. 48.

[3001] Ps. lxxxix. [lxxxviii.] 31, 32.

[3002] S. Luke xii. 47, 48.

[3003] Heb. xii. 6.

[3004] Ps. cxviii. [cxvii.] 18.

Chapter XIII.
They who have committed a "sin unto death" are not to be abandoned, but subjected to penance, according to St. Paul. Explanation of the phrase "Deliver unto Satan." Satan can afflict the body, but these afflictions bring spiritual profit, showing the power of God, Who thus turns Satan's devices against himself.

59. Lastly, Paul teaches us that we must not abandon those who have committed a sin unto death, but that we must rather coerce them with the bread of tears and tears to drink, yet so that their sorrow itself be moderated. For this is the meaning of the passage: "Thou hast given them to drink in large measure," [3005] that their sorrow itself should have its measure, lest perchance he who is doing penance should be consumed by overmuch sorrow, as was said to the Corinthians: "What will ye? Shall I come to you with a rod, or in love and a spirit of meekness?" [3006] But even the rod is not severe, since he had read: "Thou shalt beat him indeed with the rod, but shalt deliver his soul from death." [3007]

60. What the Apostle means by the rod is shown by his invective against fornication, [3008] his denunciation of incest, his reprehension of pride, because they were puffed up who ought rather to be mourning, and lastly, his sentence on the guilty person, that he should be excluded from communion, and delivered to the adversary, not for the destruction of the soul but of the flesh. For as the Lord did not give power to Satan over the soul of holy Job, but allowed him to afflict his body, [3009] so here, too, the sinner is delivered to Satan for the destruction of the flesh, that the serpent might lick the dust [3010] of his flesh, but not hurt his soul.

61. Let, then, our flesh die to lusts, let it be captive, let it be subdued, and not war against the law of our mind, but die in subjection to a good service, as in Paul, who buffeted his body that he might bring it into subjection, in order that his preaching might become more approved, if the law of his flesh agreed and was consonant with the law of his flesh. For the flesh dies when its wisdom passes over into the spirit, so that it no longer has a taste for the things of the flesh, but for the things of the spirit. Would that I might see my flesh growing weak, would that I were not dragged captive into the law of sin, would that I lived not in the flesh, but in the faith of Christ! And so there is greater grace in the infirmity of the body than in its soundness.

62. Having explained Paul's meaning, let us now consider the words themselves, in what sense he said that he had delivered him to Satan for the destruction of the flesh, for the devil it is who tries us. For he brings ailments on each of our limbs, and sickness on our whole bodies. And then, too, he smote holy Job with evil sores from the feet to the head, because he had received the power of destroying his flesh, when God said: "Behold, I give him up unto thee, only preserve his life." [3011] This the Apostle took up in the same words, giving up this man to Satan for the destruction of the flesh, that his spirit might be saved in the day of our Lord Jesus Christ. [3012]

63. Great is the power, great is the gift, which commands the devil to destroy himself. For he destroys himself when he makes the man whom he is seeking to overthrow by temptation stronger instead of weak, because whilst he is weakening the body he is strengthening his soul. For sickness of the body restrains sin, but luxury sets on fire the sin of the flesh.

64. The devil is then deceived so as to wound himself with his own bite, and to arm against himself him whom he thought to weaken. So he armed holy Job the more after he wounded him, who, with his whole body covered with sores, endured indeed the bite of the devil, but felt not his poison. And so it is well said of him, "Thou shalt draw out the dragon with an hook, thou wilt play with him as with a bird, thou shalt bind him as a boy doth a sparrow, thou shalt lay thine hand upon him." [3013]

65. You see how he is mocked by Paul, so that, like the child in prophecy, he lays his hand on the hole of the asp, and the serpent injures him not; he draws him out of his hiding-places, and makes of his venom a spiritual antidote, so that what is venom becomes a medicine, the venom serves to the destruction of the flesh, it becomes medicine to the healing of the spirit. For that which hurts the body benefits the spirit.

66. Let, then, the serpent bite the earthy part of me, let him drive his tooth into my flesh, and bruise my body; and may the Lord say of me: "I give him up unto thee, only preserve his life." How great is the power of Christ, that the guardianship of man is made a charge even to the devil himself, who always desires to injure him. Let us then make the Lord Jesus favourable to ourselves. At the command of Christ the devil himself becomes the guardian of his prey. Even unwillingly he carries out the commands of heaven, and, though cruel, obeys the commands of gentleness.

67. But why do I commend his obedience? Let him be ever evil that God may be ever good, Who converts his ill-will into grace for us. He wishes to injure us, but cannot if Christ resist him. He wounds the flesh but preserves the life. And then it is

written: "Then shall the wolves and the lambs feed together, the lion and the ox shall eat straw, and they shall not hurt nor destroy in My holy mountain, saith the Lord." [3014] For this is the sentence of condemnation on the serpent: "Dust shall be thy food." [3015] What dust? Surely that of which it is said: "Dust thou art, and into dust shalt thou return." [3016]

[3005] Ps. lxxx. [lxxix.] 5.

[3006] 1 Cor. iv. 21.

[3007] Prov. xxiii. 13.

[3008] 1 Cor. v. 1 ff.

[3009] Job ii. 6.

[3010] Mic. vii. 17.

[3011] Job ii. 6.

[3012] 1 Cor. v. 5.

[3013] Job xli. 1, 5, 8 [LXX.].

[3014] Isa. xi. 6, 8, 9.

[3015] Gen. iii. 14.

[3016] Gen. iii. 19.

Chapter XIV.
St. Ambrose explains that the flesh given to Satan for destruction is eaten by the serpent when the soul is set free from carnal desires. He gives, therefore, various rules for guarding the senses, points out the snares laid for us by means

of pleasures, and exhorts his hearers not to fear the destruction of the flesh by the serpent.

68. The serpent eats this dust, if the Lord Jesus is favourable to us, that our spirit may not sympathize with the weakness of the flesh, nor be set on fire by the vapours of the flesh and the heat of our members. "It is better to marry than to burn," [3017] for there is a flame which burns within. Let us not then suffer this fire to approach the bosom of our minds and the depths of our hearts, lest we burn up the covering of our inmost hearts, and lest the devouring fire of lust consume this outward garment of the soul and its fleshy veil, but let us pass through the fire. [3018] And should any one fall into the fire of love let him leap over it and pass forth; let him not bind to himself adulterous lust with the bands of thoughts, let him not tie knots around himself by the fastenings of continual reflection, let him not too often turn his attention to the form of a harlot, and let not a maiden lift her eyes to the countenance of a youth. And if by chance she has looked and is caught, how much more will she be entangled if she gazes with curiosity.

69. Let custom itself teach us. A woman covers her face with a veil for this reason, that in public her modesty may be safe. That her face may not easily meet the gaze of a youth, let her be covered with the nuptial veil, so that not even in chance meetings she might be exposed to the wounding of another or of herself, though the wound of either were indeed hers. But if she cover her head with a veil that she may not accidentally see or be seen (for when the head is veiled the face is hidden), how much more ought she to cover herself with the veil of modesty, so as even in public to have her own secret place.

70. But granted that the eye has fallen upon another, at least let not the inward affection follow. For to have seen is no sin, but one must be careful that it be not the source of sin. The bodily eye sees, but let the eye of the heart be closed; let modesty of mind remain. We have a Lord Who is both strict and indulgent. The prophet indeed said: "Look not upon the beauty of a woman that is all harlot." [3019] But the Lord said: "Whoever shall look on a woman to lust after her, hath committed adultery with her already in his heart." [3020] He does not say, "Whosoever shall look hath committed adultery," but "Whosoever shall look on her to lust after her." He condemned not the look but sought out the inward affection. But that modesty is praiseworthy which has so accustomed itself to close the bodily eyes as often not to see what we really behold. For we seem to behold with the bodily sight whatever meets us; but if there be not joined to this any attention of the mind, the sight also, according to what is usual in the body, fades away, so that in reality we see rather with the mind than with the body.

71. And if the flesh has seen the flame, let us not cherish that flame in our bosoms, that is, in the depths of the heart and the inward part of the mind. Let us not instil this fire into our bones, let us not bind bonds upon ourselves, let us not join in conversation with such as may be the cause to us of unholy fires. The speech of a maiden is a snare to a youth, the words of a youth are the bonds of love.

72. Joseph saw the fire when the woman eager for adultery spoke to him. [3021] She wished to catch him with her words. She set the snares of her lips, but was not able to capture the chaste man. For the voice of modesty, the voice of gravity, the rein of caution, the care for integrity, the discipline of chastity, loosed the woman's chains. So that unchaste person could not

entangle him in her meshes. She laid her hand upon him; she caught his garment, that she might tighten the noose around him. The words of a lascivious woman are the snares of lust, and her hands the bonds of love; but the chaste mind could not be taken either by snares or by bonds. The garment was cast off, the bonds were loosed, and because he did not admit the fire into the bosom of his mind, his body was not burnt.

73. You see, then, that our mind is the cause of our guilt. And so the flesh is innocent, but is often the minister of sin. Let not, then, desire of beauty overcome you. Many nets and many snares are spread by the devil. The look of a harlot is the snare of him who loves her. Our own eyes are nets to us, wherefore it is written: "Be not taken with thine eyes." [3022] So, then, we spread nets for ourselves in which we are entangled and hampered. We bind chains on ourselves, as we read: "For every one is bound with the chains of his own sins." [3023]

74. Let us then pass through the fires of youth and the glow of early years; let us pass through the waters, let us not remain therein, lest the deep floods shut us in. Let us rather pass over, that we too may say: "Our soul has passed over the stream," [3024] for he who has passed over is safe. And lastly, the Lord speaks thus: "If thou pass through the water, I am with thee, the rivers shall not overflow thee." [3025] And the prophet says: "I have seen the wicked exalted above the cedars of Libanus, and I passed by, and lo, he was not." Pass by things of this world, and you will see that the high places of the wicked have fallen. Moses, too, passing by things of this world, saw a great sight and said: "I will turn aside and see this great sight," [3026] for had he been held by the fleeting pleasures of this world he would not have seen so great a mystery.

75. Let us also pass over this fire of lust, fearing which Paul--but fearing for us, inasmuch as by buffeting his body he had come no longer to fear for himself--says to us: "Flee fornication." [3027] Let us then flee it as though following us, though indeed it follows not behind us, but within our very selves. Let us then diligently take heed lest while we are fleeing from it we carry it with ourselves. For we wish for the most part to flee, but if we do not wholly cast it out of our mind, we rather take it up than forsake it. Let us then spring over it, lest it be said to us: "Walk ye in the flame of your fire, which ye have kindled for yourselves." [3028] For as he who "takes fire into his bosom burns his clothes," [3029] so he who walks upon fiery coals must of necessity burn his feet, as it is written: "Can one walk upon coals of fire and not burn his feet?" [3030]

76. This fire is dangerous, let us then not feed it with the fuel of luxury. Lust is fed by feastings, nourished by delicacies, kindled by wine, and inflamed by drunkenness. Still more dangerous than these are the incentives of words, which intoxicate the mind as it were with a kind of wine of the vine of Sodom. Let us be on our guard against abundance of this wine, for when the flesh is intoxicated the mind totters, the heart wavers, the heart is carried to and fro. And so with regard to each that precept is useful wherein Timothy is warned: "Drink a little wine because of thy frequent infirmities." [3031] When the body is heated, it excites the glow of the mind; when the flesh is chilled with the cold of disease the spirit is chilled; when the body is in pain, the mind is sad, but the sadness shall become joy.

77. Do not then fear if your flesh be eaten away, the soul is not consumed. And so David says that he does not fear, because the enemy were eating up his flesh but not his soul, as we read:

"When evil-doers come near upon me to eat up my flesh, my foes who trouble me, they were weakened and fell." [3032] So the serpent works overthrow for himself alone, therefore is he who has been injured by the serpent given over to the serpent that he may raise up again him whom he cast down, and the overthrow of the serpent may be the raising again of the man. And Scripture testifies that Satan is the author of this bodily suffering and weakness of the flesh, where Paul says: "There was given unto me a thorn in the flesh, a messenger of Satan to buffet me, that I should not be exalted." [3033] So Paul learned to heal even as he himself had been made whole.

[3017] 1 Cor. vii. 9; Prov. vi. 27.

[3018] Isa. xliii. 2.

[3019] Possibly from Prov. v. condensed.

[3020] S. Matt. v. 28.

[3021] Gen. xxxix. 7.

[3022] Prov. vi. 25.

[3023] Prov. vi. 2 [LXX.] very loosely.

[3024] Ps. cxxiv. [cxxiii.] 4.

[3025] Isa. xliii. 2.

[3026] Ex. iii. 3.

[3027] 1 Cor. vi. 18.

[3028] Isa. l. 11.

[3029] Prov. vi. 27.

[3030] Prov. vi. 28.

[3031] 1 Tim. v. 23.

[3032] Ps. xxvii. 2.

[3033] 2 Cor. xii. 7.

Chapter XV.
Returning from this digression, St. Ambrose explains what is the meaning of St. Paul where he speaks of coming "with a rod or in the spirit of meekness."One who has grievously fallen is to be separated, but to be again restored to religious privileges when he has sufficiently repented. The old leaven is purged out when the hardness of the letter is tempered by the meal of a milder interpretation. All should be sprinkled with the Church's meal and fed with the food of charity, lest they become like that envious elder brother, whose example is followed by the Novatians.

78. That faithful teacher, having promised one of two things, gave each. He came with a rod, for he separated the guilty man from the holy fellowship. And well is he said to be delivered to Satan who is separated from the body of Christ. But he came in love and with the spirit of meekness, whether because he so delivered him up as to save his soul, or because he afterwards restored to the sacraments him whom he had before separated.

79. For it is needful to separate one who has grievously fallen, lest a little leaven corrupt the whole lump. And the old leaven must be purged out, or the old man in each person; that is, the outward man and his deeds, he who among the people has grown old in sin and hardened in vices. And well did he say purged, not cast forth, for what is purged is not considered wholly valueless, for to this end is it purged, that what is of

value be separated from the worthless, but that which is cast forth is considered to have in itself nothing of value.

80. The Apostle then judged that the sinner should then at once be restored to the heavenly sacraments if he himself wished to be cleansed. And well is it said "Purge," for he is purged as by certain things done by the whole people, and is washed in the tears of the multitude, and redeemed from sin by the weeping of the multitude, and is purged in the inner man. For Christ granted to His Church that one should be redeemed by means of all, as she herself was found worthy of the coming of the Lord Jesus, in order that through One all might be redeemed.

81. This is Paul's meaning which the words make more obscure. Let us consider the exact words of the Apostle: "Purge out," says he, "the old leaven, that ye may be a new lump, even as ye are unleavened." [3034] Either that the whole Church takes up the burden of the sinner, with whom she has to suffer in weeping and prayer and pain, and, as it were, covers herself with his leaven, in order that by means of all that which is to be done away in the individual doing penance may be purged by a kind of contribution and commixture of compassion and mercy offered with manly vigor. [3035] Or one may understand it as that woman in the Gospel teaches us, who is a type of the Church, when she hid the leaven in her meal, till all was leavened, and the whole could be used as pure.

82. The Lord taught me in the Gospel what leaven is when He said: "Do ye not understand that I said not concerning bread, Beware of the leaven of the Pharisees and Sadducees?" [3036] Then, it is said, they understood that He spake not of bread, but that they should beware of the doctrine of the Pharisees

and Sadducees. This leaven, then--that is, the doctrine of the Pharisees and the contentiousness of the Sadducees--the Church hides in her meal, when she softened the hard letter of the Law by a spiritual interpretation, and ground it as it were in the mill of her explanations, bringing out as it were from the husks of the letter the inner secrets of the mysteries, and setting forth the belief in the Resurrection, wherein the mercy of God is proclaimed, and wherein it is believed that the life of those who are dead is restored.

83. Now this comparison seems to be not unfitly brought forward in this place, since the kingdom of heaven is redemption from sin, and therefore we all, both bad and good, are mingled with the meal of the Church that we all may be a new lump. But that no one may be afraid that an admixture of evil leaven might injure the lump, the Apostle said: "That ye may be a new lump, even as ye are unleavened;" [3037] that is to say, This mixture will render you again such, as in the pure integrity of your innocence. If we thus have compassion, we are not stained with the sins of others, but we gain the restoration of another to the increase of our own grace, so that our integrity remains as it was. And therefore he adds: "For Christ our Passover is sacrificed for us; " [3038] that is, the Passion of the Lord profited all, and gave redemption to sinners who repented of the sins they had committed.

84. Let us then keep the feast on good food, doing penance yet joyful in our redemption, for no food is sweeter than kindness and gentleness. Let no envy towards the sinner who is saved be mingled with our feasts and joy, lest that envious brother, as is set forth in the Gospel, exclude himself from the house of his Father, because he grieved at the reception of his brother, at whose lasting exile he was wont to rejoice.

85. And you Novatians cannot deny that you are like him, who, as you say, do not come together to the Church because by penance a hope of return had been given to those who had lapsed. But this is only a pretence, for Novatian contrived his schism through grief at his loss of the episcopal office.

86. But do you not understand that the Apostle also prophesied of you and says to you: "And ye are puffed up and did not rather mourn, that he who did this deed might be taken away from among you"? [3039] He is, then, wholly taken away when his sin is done away, but the Apostle does not say that the sinner is to be shut out of the Church who counsels his cleansing.

[3034] 1 Cor. v. 7.

[3035] There is probably here a reference to a generous custom of antiquity, whereby if any one were visited by calamity and loss of goods, his friends contributed according to their power to present him with a gift which should help to re-establish him. St. Ambrose seems to apply this to the bearing one another's burdens by mourning, fasting, and praying with the penitent, that God might be moved by the entreaties of all, offered with great energy, and forgive what might be lacking in the individual. It is an instructive commentary on the doctrine of the communion of saints.

[3036] S. Matt. xvi. 11.

[3037] 1 Cor. v. 7.

[3038] 1 Cor. v. 7.

[3039] 1 Cor. v. 2.

Chapter XVI.

Comparison between the apostles and Novatians. The fitness of the words, "Ye know not what spirit ye are of," when applied to them. The desire of penance is extinguished by them when they take away its fruit. And thus are sinners deprived of the promises of Christ, though, indeed, they ought not to be too soon admitted to the mysteries. Some examples of repentance.

87. Inasmuch, then, as the Apostle forgave sins, by what authority do you say that they are not to be forgiven? Who has the most reverence for Christ, Paul or Novatian? But Paul knew that the Lord was merciful. He knew that the Lord Jesus was offended more by the harshness of the disciples than by their pitifulness.

88. Furthermore, Jesus rebuked James and John when they spoke of bringing down fire from heaven to consume those who refused to receive the Lord, and said to them: "Ye know not whose spirit ye are of; for the Son of Man is not come to destroy men's lives but to save them." [3040] To them, indeed, He said, "Ye know not whose spirit ye are of," who were of His spirit; but to you He says, "Ye are not of My spirit, who hold not fast My clemency, who reject My mercy, who refuse repentance which I willed to be preached by the apostles in My Name."

89. For it is in vain that you say that you preach repentance who remove the fruits of repentance. For men are led to the pursuit of anything either by rewards or results, and every pursuit grows slack by delay. And for this reason the Lord, in order that the devotion of His disciples might be increased, said that every one who had left all that was his, and followed God, should receive sevenfold more both here and hereafter. [3041] First of all He promised the reward here, to do away with the

tedium of delay, and again hereafter, that we might learn to believe that rewards will also be given to us hereafter. Present rewards are then an earnest of those hereafter.

90. If, then, any one, having committed hidden sins, shall nevertheless diligently do penance, how shall he receive those rewards if not restored to the communion of the Church? I am willing, indeed, that the guilty man should hope for pardon, should seek it with tears and groans, should seek it with the aid of the tears of all the people, should implore forgiveness; and if communion be postponed two or three times, that he should believe that his entreaties have not been urgent enough, that he must increase his tears, must come again even in greater trouble, clasp the feet of the faithful with his arms, kiss them, wash them with tears, and not let them go, so that the Lord Jesus may say of him too: "His sins which are many are forgiven, for he loved much." [3042]

91. I have known penitents whose countenance was furrowed with tears, their cheeks worn with constant weeping, who offered their body to be trodden under foot by all, who with faces ever pale and worn with fasting bore about in a yet living body the likeness of death.

[3040] S. Luke ix. 55, 56.

[3041] S. Matt. xix. 29.

[3042] S. Luke vii. 47.

Chapter XVII.
That gentleness must be added to severity, as is shown in the case of St. Paul at Corinth. The man had been baptized, though the Novatians argue against it. And by the word "destruction" is not meant annihilation but severe chastening.

92. Why do we postpone the time of pardon for those who have mortified themselves, who during life have done themselves to death? "Sufficient," says St. Paul, "to such a one is this punishment which is inflicted by the many; so that contrariwise, ye should rather forgive him and comfort him, lest by any means he should be swallowed up with overmuch sorrow." [3043] If the punishment which is inflicted by the many is sufficient for condemnation, the intercession which is made by many is also sufficient for the remission of sin. The Master of morals, Who both knows our weakness and is the interpreter of the will of God, wills that comfort should be given, lest sorrow through the weariness of long delay should swallow up the penitent.

93. The Apostle then forgave him, and not only forgave him, but desired that love to him should again grow strong. He who is loved receives not harshness but mercy. And not only did he himself forgive him only, but willed that all should forgive him, and says that he forgave for the sake of others, lest many should be longer saddened on account of one. "To whom," says he, "ye have forgiven anything, I forgive also, for I also have forgiven for your sakes in the person of Christ, for we are not ignorant of his devices." [3044] Rightly can he be on his guard against the serpent who is not ignorant of his devices, of which there are so many to our detriment. He is always desirous to do harm, always desirous to circumvent us, that he may cause death; but we ought to take heed lest our remedy

94

become an occasion of triumph for him; for we are circumvented by him, if any one perish through overmuch sorrow, who might be set free by pitifulness.

94. And that we may know that this person was baptized, he added: "I wrote to you in my epistle to have no company with fornicators, not altogether with fornicators of this world." [3045] And farther on he adds: "But now I write unto you not to keep company if any man that is named a brother be a fornicator, or covetous, or an idolator." [3046] Those whom he has joined together under one penalty, he willed to attain together to forgiveness. "If any be such," he says, "with him not to eat." [3047] How severe he is with the obstinate, how indulgent to those who seek. Against those rises up in arms the injury done to Christ, whilst the calling upon Christ aids these.

95. But lest any one be perplexed because it is written: "I have delivered such an one unto Satan for the destruction of the flesh," [3048] and should say: How can he attain forgiveness whose whole flesh has perished, seeing that it is evident that man was redeemed both in body and soul, and is saved in both and that neither the soul without the body, nor yet the body without the soul, since both are united by their fellowship in the deeds that have been done, can be without fellowship either in punishment or in reward? Let this suffice for an answer to him: That "destruction" does not mean the complete annihilation of the flesh, but its chastening. For as he who is dead to sin lives to God, so the allurements of the flesh perish, and the flesh dies to its lusts, in order that it may live again to purity and to other good works.

96. And what more suitable example can we take than one from our common mother? For the earth itself, from which we

are all taken, when it is not worked and cultivated, seems to be desert; and the field dies to the vines or olive-trees with which it was planted, and yet it does not lose its own nutritive power, which is, as it were, its life. And then later, when cultivation begins once more, and the seed is sown for which the land seems suitable, it breaks forth again more fruitful than before with its products. It is not, then, anything so strange if our flesh is said to die, and yet is understood to be subdued rather than annihilated.

[3043] 2 Cor. ii. 6.

[3044] 2 Cor. ii. 10.

[3045] 1 Cor. v. 9.

[3046] 1 Cor. v. 11.

[3047] 1 Cor. v. 11.

[3048] 1 Cor. v. 5.

Book II.

Chapter I.
St. Ambrose gives additional rules concerning repentance, and shows that it must not be delayed.

1. Although in the former book we have written many things which may tend to the more perfect practice of repentance, yet inasmuch as a great deal more may be added, we will continue the repast so as not to seem to have relinquished the provisions of our teaching only half consumed.

2. For repentance must be taken in hand not only anxiously, but also quickly, lest perchance that father of the house in the Gospel who planted a fig-tree in his vineyard should come and seek fruit on it, and finding none, say to the vine-dresser: "Cut it down, why doth it cumber the ground?" [3049] And unless the vine-dresser should intercede and say: "Lord, let it alone this year also, until I dig about it and dung it, and if it bear fruit-well; but if not let it be cut down." [3050]

3. Let us then dung this field which we possess, and imitate those hard-working farmers, who are not ashamed to satiate the land with rich dung and to scatter the grimy ashes over the field, that they may gather more abundant crops.

4. And the Apostle teaches us how to dung it, saying: "I count all things but dung, that I may gain Christ," [3051] and he, through evil report and good report, attained to pleasing Christ. For he had read that Abraham, when confessing himself to be but dust and ashes, [3052] in his deep humility found favour with God. He had read how Job, sitting among the ashes, [3053] regained all that he had lost. [3054] He had heard in the

utterance of David, how God "raiseth the poor out of the dust, and lifteth the needy out of the dunghill." [3055]

5. Let us then not be ashamed to confess our sins unto the Lord. Shame indeed there is when each makes known his sins, but that shame, as it were, ploughs his land, removes the ever-recurring brambles, prunes the thorns, and gives life to the fruits which he believed were dead. Follow him who, by diligently ploughing his field, sought for eternal fruit: "Being reviled we bless, being persecuted we endure, being defamed we entreat, we are made as the offscouring of the world." [3056] If you plough after this fashion you will sow spiritual seed. Plough that you may get rid of sin and gain fruit. He ploughed so as to destroy in himself the last tendency to persecution. What more could Christ give to lead us on to the pursuit of perfection, than to convert and then give us for a teacher one who was a persecutor?

[3049] S. Luke xiii. 7.

[3050] S. Luke xiii. 8, 9.

[3051] Phil. iii. 8.

[3052] Gen. xviii. 27.

[3053] Job ii. 8.

[3054] Job xlii. 10.

[3055] Ps. cxiii. [cxii.] 7.

[3056] 1 Cor. iv. 12, 13.

Chapter II.
A passage quoted by the heretics against repentance is

explained in two ways, the first being that Heb. vi. 4 refers to the impossibility of being baptized again; the second, that what is impossible with man is possible with God.

6. Being then refuted by the clear example of the Apostle and by his writings, the heretics yet endeavour to resist further, and say that their opinion is supported by apostolic authority, bringing forward the passage in the Epistle to the Hebrews: "For it is impossible that those who were once enlightened, and have tasted the heavenly gift, and have been made partakers of the Holy Spirit, and have tasted the good word of God, and the powers of the world to come, should if they fall away be again renewed unto repentance, crucifying again the Son of God, and put Him to open shame." [3057]

7. Could Paul teach in opposition to his own act? He had at Corinth forgiven sin through penance, how could he himself speak against his own decision? Since, then, he could not destroy what he had built, we must assume that what he says was different from, but not contrary to, what had gone before. For what is contrary is opposed to itself, what is different has ordinarily another meaning. Things which are contrary are not such that one can support the other. Inasmuch, then, as the Apostle spoke of remitting penance, he could not be silent as to those who thought that baptism was to be repeated. And it was right first of all to remove our anxiety, and to let us know that even after baptism, if any sinned their sins could be forgiven them, lest a false belief in a reiterated baptism should lead astray those who were destitute of all hope of forgiveness. And secondly, it was right to set forth in a well-reasoned argument that baptism is not to be repeated.

8. And that the writer was speaking of baptism is evident from the very words in which it is stated that it is impossible to renew unto repentance those who were fallen, inasmuch as we are renewed by means of the laver of baptism, whereby we are born again, as Paul says himself: "For we are buried with Him through baptism into death, that, like as Christ rose from the dead through the glory of the Father, so we, too, should walk in newness of life." [3058] And in another place: "Be ye renewed in the spirit of your mind, and put on the new man which is created after God." [3059] And elsewhere again: "Thy youth shall be renewed like the eagle," [3060] because the eagle after death is born again from its ashes, as we being dead in sin are through the Sacrament of Baptism born again to God, and created anew. So, then, here as elsewhere, he teaches one baptism. "One faith," he says, "one baptism." [3061]

9. This, too, is plain, that in him who is baptized the Son of God is crucified, for our flesh could not do away sin unless it were crucified in Jesus Christ. And then it is written that: "All we who were baptized into Jesus Christ were baptized into His death." [3062] And farther on: "If we have been planted in the likeness of His death, we shall be also in the likeness of His resurrection, knowing that our old man was fastened with Him to His cross." [3063] And to the Colossians he says: "Buried with Him by baptism, wherein ye also rose again with Him." [3064] Which was written to the intent that we should believe that He is crucified in us, that our sins may be purged through Him, that He, Who alone can forgive sins, may nail to His cross the handwriting which was against us. [3065] In us He triumphs over principalities and powers, as it is written of Him: "He made a show of principalities and powers, triumphing over them in Himself." [3066]

10. So, then, that which he says in this Epistle to the Hebrews, that it is impossible for those who have fallen to be "renewed unto repentance, crucifying again the Son of God, and putting Him to open shame," must be considered as having reference to baptism, wherein we crucify the Son of God in ourselves, that the world may be by Him crucified for us, who triumph, as it were, when we take to ourselves the likeness of His death, who put to open shame upon His cross principalities and powers, and triumphed over them, that in the likeness of His death we, too, might triumph over the principalities whose yoke we throw off. But Christ was crucified once, and died to sin once, and so there is but one, not several baptisms.

11. But what of the passage wherein the doctrine of baptisms is spoken of? Because under the Law there were many baptisms or washings, he rightly rebukes those who forsake what is perfect and seek again the first principles of the word. He teaches us that the whole of the washings under the Law are done away with, and that there is one baptism in the sacraments of the Church. But he exhorts us that leaving the first principles of the word we should go on to perfection. "And this," he says, "we will do, if God permits," [3067] for no one can be perfect without the grace of God.

12. And indeed I might also say to any one who thought that this passage spoke of repentance, that things which are impossible with men are possible with God; and God is able whensoever He wills to forgive us our sins, even those which we think cannot be forgiven. And so it is possible for God to give us that which it seems to us impossible to obtain. For it seemed impossible that water should wash away sin, and Naaman the Syrian [3068] thought that his leprosy could not be cleansed by water. But that which was impossible God made to

be possible, Who gave us so great grace. In like manner it seemed impossible that sins should be forgiven through repentance, but Christ gave this power to His apostles, which has been transmitted to the priestly office. That, then, has become possible which was impossible. But, by a true reasoning, he convinces us that the reiteration by any one of the Sacrament of Baptism is not permitted.

[3057] Heb. vi. 4-6. The use made by the Montanists and Novatians of this passage in support of their heresy seems to have been one of the reasons why the Epistle to the Hebrews was so late in being received as canonical. This is stated by one authority in so many words: "Epistola ad Hebraeos non legitur propter Novatianos." Philastrius, de Haer. 41.

[3058] Rom. vi. 4.

[3059] Eph. iv. 23.

[3060] Ps. civ. [ciii.] 5.

[3061] Eph. iv. 5.

[3062] Rom. vi. 3.

[3063] Rom. vi. 5, 6.

[3064] Col. ii. 12.

[3065] Col. ii. 14.

[3066] Col. ii. 15.

[3067] Heb. vi. 3.

[3068] 2 [4] Kings v. 11.

Chapter III.
Explanation of the parable of the Prodigal Son, in which St. Ambrose applies it to refute the teaching of the Novatians, proving that reconciliation ought not to be refused to the greatest offender upon suitable proof of repentance.

13. And the Apostle does not contradict the plain teaching of Christ, Who set forth, as a comparison of a repentant sinner, one going to a foreign country after receiving all his substance from his father, wasted it in riotous living, and later, when feeding upon husks, longed for his father's bread and then gained the robe, the ring, the shoes, and the slaying of the calf, [3069] which is a likeness of the Passion of the Lord, whereby we receive forgiveness.

14. Well is it said that he went into a foreign country who is cut off from the sacred altar, for this is to be separated from that Jerusalem which is in heaven, from the citizenship and home of the saints. For which reason the Apostle says: "Therefore now ye are no more strangers and foreigners, but fellow-citizens with the saints and of the household of God." [3070]

15. "And," it is said, "wasted his substance." Rightly, for he whose faith halts in bringing forth good works does consume it. For, "faith is the substance of things hoped for, the evidence of things not seen." [3071] And faith is a good substance, the inheritance of our hope.

16. And no wonder if he was perishing for hunger, who lacked the divine nourishment, impelled by the want of which he says: "I will arise and go to my father, and will say unto him: Father, I have sinned against heaven, and before thee." Do you not see it plainly declared to us, that we are urged to prayer for the sake of gaining the sacrament? and do you wish to take away that for

the sake of which penance is undertaken? Deprive the pilot of
the hope of reaching port, and he will wander uncertainly here
and there on the waves. Take away the crown from the athlete,
and he will fail and lie on the course. Take from the fisher the
power of catching his booty, and he will cease to cast the nets.
How, then, can he, who suffers hunger in his soul, pray more
earnestly to God, if he has no hope of the heavenly food?

17. "I have sinned," he says, "against heaven, and before thee."
He confesses what is clearly a sin unto death, that you may not
think that any one doing penance [3072] is rightly shut out
from pardon. For he who has sinned against heaven has sinned
either against the kingdom of heaven, or against his own soul,
which is a sin unto death, and against God, to Whom alone is
said: "Against Thee only have I sinned, and done evil before
Thee." [3073]

18. So quickly does he gain forgiveness, that, as he is coming,
and is still a great way off, his father meets him, gives him a
kiss, which is the sign of sacred peace; orders the robe to be
brought forth, which is the marriage garment, which if any one
have not, he is shut out from the marriage feast; places the ring
on his hand, which is the pledge of faith and the seal of the
Holy Spirit; orders the shoes to be brought out, [3074] for he
who is about to celebrate the Lord's Passover, about to feast on
the Lamb, ought to have his feet protected against all attacks of
spiritual wild beasts and the bite of the serpent; bids the calf to
be slain, for "Christ our Passover hath been sacrificed." [3075]
For as often as we receive the Blood of the Lord, we proclaim
the death of the Lord. [3076] As, then, He was once slain for
all, so whensoever forgiveness of sins is granted, we receive the
Sacrament of His Body, that through His Blood there may be
remission of sins.

104

19. Therefore most evidently are we bidden by the teaching of the Lord to confer again the grace of the heavenly sacrament on those guilty even of the greatest sins, if they with open confession bear the penance due to their sin.

[3069] S. Luke xv. 13 ff.

[3070] Eph. ii. 19.

[3071] Heb. xi. 1.

[3072] Penitentiam agere must here and elsewhere be translated thus, for it implies not mere repentance, but the undergoing outward discipline. The word penitentia means both repentance and penance.

[3073] Ps. li. [l.] 4.

[3074] Ex. xii. 11.

[3075] 1 Cor. v. 7.

[3076] 1 Cor. xi. 26.

Chapter IV.
St. Ambrose turns against the Novatians themselves another objection concerning blasphemy against the Holy Spirit, showing that it consists in an erroneous belief, proving this by St. Peter's words against Simon Magus, and other passages, exhorting the Novatians to return to the Church, affirming that such is our Lord's mercy that even Judas would have found forgiveness had he repented.

20. But we have heard that you are accustomed to bring forward as an objection that which is written: "Every sin and blasphemy shall be forgiven unto men, but blasphemies against

the Spirit shall not be forgiven unto men. And whosoever shall speak a word against the Son of Man, it shall be forgiven him, but whosoever shall speak against the Holy Spirit, it shall not be forgiven him, neither in this world, nor in that which is to come." [3077] By which quotation the whole of your assertion is destroyed and done away, for it is written: "Every sin and blasphemy shall be forgiven unto men." Why, then, do you not remit them? Why do you bind chains which you do not loose? Why do you tie knots which you do not unfasten? Forgive the others, and deal with those who you think are bound for ever by the authority of the Gospel for sinning against the Holy Spirit.

21. But let us consider the case of those whom the Lord so binds, going back to the words before the passage quoted, that we may understand it more clearly: The Jews were saying: "This man doth not cast out devils, but by Beelzebub, prince of the devils." Jesus replied: "Every kingdom divided against itself shall be destroyed, and every city or house divided against itself shall not stand; for if Satan casteth out Satan, he is divided against himself, how then shall his kingdom stand? But if I cast out devils by Beelzebub, by whom do your sons cast them out?" [3078]

22. Now we see plainly here that the words are expressly used of those who were saying that the Lord Jesus cast out devils through Beelzebub, to whom the Lord gave that answer, because they were of the heritage of Satan, who compared the Saviour of all to Satan, and attributed the grace of Christ to the kingdom of the devil. And that we might know that He was speaking of this blasphemy, He added: "O generation of vipers, how can ye speak good, being yourselves evil?" He says, then, that those who thus speak attain not to forgiveness.

23. Then, when Simon, depraved by long practice of magic, had thought he could gain by money the power of conferring the grace of Christ and the infusion of the Holy Spirit, Peter said: "Thou hast neither part nor lot in this faith, for thy heart is not right with God. Repent therefore of this thy wickedness, and pray the Lord, if perchance this thought of thy heart may be forgiven thee, for I see that thou art in the bond of iniquity and in the bitterness of gall." [3079] We see that Peter by his apostolic authority condemns him who blasphemes against the Holy Spirit through magic vanity, and all the more because he had not the clear consciousness of faith. And yet he did not exclude him from the hope of forgiveness, for he called him to repentance.

24. The Lord then replies to the blasphemy of the Pharisees, and refuses to them the grace of His power, which consists in the remission of sins, because they asserted that His heavenly power rested on the help of the devil. And He affirms that they act with satanic spirit who divide the Church of God, so that He includes the heretics and schismatics of all times, to whom He denies forgiveness, for every other sin is concerned with single persons, this is a sin against all. For they alone wish to destroy the grace of Christ who rend asunder the members of the Church for which the Lord Jesus suffered, and the Holy Spirit was given us.

25. Lastly, that we may know that He is speaking of those who destroy the unity of the Church, we find it written: "He that is not with Me is against Me, and he that gathered not with Me, scattereth." [3080] And that we might know that He is speaking of these, He at once added: "Therefore I say unto you, every sin and blasphemy shall be forgiven unto men, but blasphemies against the Spirit shall not be forgiven unto men." When He

says, "Therefore say I unto you," is it not evident that He intended the words following to be laid to heart by us beyond the others? And He rightly added: "A good tree bringeth forth good fruits, but a bad tree bringeth forth bad fruits," [3081] for an evil association cannot produce good fruits. The tree, then, is the association; the fruits of the good tree are the children of the Church.

26. Return, then, to the Church, those of you who have wickedly separated yourselves. For He promises forgiveness to all who are converted, since it is written: "Whosoever shall call on the Name of the Lord shall be saved." [3082] And lastly, the Jewish people who said of the Lord Jesus, "He hath a devil," [3083] and "He casteth out devils through Beelzebub," and who crucified the Lord Jesus, are, by the preaching of Peter, called to baptism, that they may put away the guilt of so great a wickedness.

27. But what wonder is it if you should deny salvation to others, who reject your own, though they lose nothing who seek for penance from you? For I suppose that even Judas might through the exceeding mercy of God not have been shut out from forgiveness, if he had expressed his sorrow not before the Jews but before Christ. "I have sinned," he said, "in that I have betrayed righteous blood." [3084] Their answer was: "What is that to us, see thou to that." What other reply do you give, when one guilty of a smaller sin confesses his deed to you? What do you answer but this: "What is that to us, see thou to that"? The halter followed on those words, but the punishment is all the more severe, the smaller the sin is.

28. But if they be not converted, do you at least repent, who by many a slip have fallen from the lofty pinnacle of innocence

and faith. We have a good Lord, Whose will it is to forgive all, Who called you by the prophet, and said: "I, even I, am He that blotteth out transgressions, and I will not remember, but do thou remember, and let us plead together." [3085]

[3077] S. Matt. xii. 31, 32.

[3078] S. Matt. xii. 24 ff.

[3079] Acts viii. 21 ff.

[3080] S. Matt. xii. 30.

[3081] S. Matt. vii. 17.

[3082] Joel ii. 32.

[3083] S. John viii. 43.

[3084] S. Matt. xxvii. 5.

[3085] Isa. xliii. 25 [LXX.]. St. Ambrose, taking the Septuagint reading, makes the contrast to be between man's remembering and God's forgetting. But the contrast in the Hebrew is different: God will do away sins of His pure mercy and challenges Israel to bring forward any merits which can plead for pardon. God shows that His mercy is even greater than His justice. St. Ambrose, as is shown more clearly in chap. vi., is merely using a verbal antithesis.

Chapter V.
As to the words of St. Peter to Simon Magus, from which the Novatians infer that there was no forgiveness for the latter, it is pointed out that St. Peter, knowing his evil heart, might well use words of doubt, and then by some Old Testament instances it is pointed out that "perchance" does not exclude forgiveness.

The apostles transmitted to us that penitence, the fruits of which are shown in the case of David. St. Ambrose then adduces the example of the Ephraimites, whose penitence must be followed in order to gain the divine mercy and the sacraments.

29. The Novatians bring up a question from the words of the Apostle Peter. Because he said, "if perchance," they think that he did not imply that forgiveness would be granted on repentance. But let them consider concerning whom the words were spoken: of Simon, who did not believe through faith, but was meditating trickery. So too the Lord to him who said, "Lord, I will follow Thee withersoever Thou goest," replied, "Foxes have holes." [3086] For He knew that the man's sincerity was not wholly perfect. If, then, the Lord refused to him who was not baptized permission to follow Him, because He saw that he was not sincere, do you wonder that the Apostle did not absolve him who after baptism was guilty of deceit, and whom he declared to be still in the bond of iniquity?

30. But let this be my answer to them. As to myself, I say that Peter did not doubt, and I do not think that so great a question can be burked by the questionable interpretation of a single word. For if they think that Peter doubted, did God doubt, Who said to the prophet Jeremiah: "Stand in the court of the Lord's house, and thou shalt give an answer to all Judah, to those who come to worship in the Lord's house, even all the words which I have appointed for thee to answer them. Keep not back a word, perchance they will hearken and be converted." [3087] Let them say, then, that God also knew not what would happen.

31. But ignorance is not implied in that word, but the common custom of holy Scripture is observed, in order to simplicity of

110

utterance. Inasmuch as the Lord says also to Ezekiel: "Son of man, I will send thee unto the house of Israel, to those who have angered Me, both themselves and their fathers, unto this day, and thou shalt say unto them, Thus saith the Lord, if perchance they will hear and be afraid." [3088] Did He not know that they could or could not be converted? So, then, that expression is not always a proof of doubt.

32. Lastly, the wise men of this world, who stake all their reputation on expressions and words, do not everywhere use the Latin word forte, "perchance," or its Greek equivalent tacha, as an expression of doubt. And so they say that their earliest poet used the words,

...e tacha chere

...esomai,

which is, "I shall soon be a widow;" and the passage goes on:

... tacha gar se katakneousin 'Achaioi

pantes ephormethentes. [3089]

But he had no doubt that when all were Joining in the attack one might well be laid low by all.

33. But let us use our own instances rather than foreign ones. You find in the Gospel that the Son Himself says of the Father (when He had sent His servants to His vineyard, and they had been slain), that the Father said, "I will send My well-beloved Son, perchance they will reverence Him." [3090] And in another place the Son says of Himself: "Ye know neither Me nor My Father; for if ye knew Me, ye would perchance know My Father also." [3091]

34. If, then, Peter used those words which were used by God without any prejudice to His knowledge, why should we not assume that Peter also used them without prejudice to his belief? For he could not doubt concerning the gift of Christ, Who had given him the power of forgiving sins; especially since he was bound not to leave any place for the craftiness of heretics who desire to deprive men of hope, in order the more easily to insinuate into the despairing their opinion as to the reiteration of baptism.

35. But the apostles, having this baptism according to the direction of Christ, taught repentance, promised forgiveness, and remitted guilt, as David taught when he said: "Blessed are they whose transgressions are forgiven, and whose sins are covered. Blessed is the man to whom the Lord hath not imputed sin." [3092] He calls each blessed, both him whose sins are remitted by the font, and him whose sin is covered by good works. For he who repents ought not only to wash away his sin by his tears, but also to cover and hide his former transgressions by amended deeds, that sin may not be imputed to him.

36. Let us, then, cover our falls by our subsequent acts; let us purify ourselves by tears, that the Lord our God may hear us when we lament, as He heard Ephraim when weeping, as it is written: "I have surely heard Ephraim weeping." [3093] And He expressly repeats the very words of Ephraim: "Thou hast chastised me and I was chastised, like a calf I was not trained." [3094] For a calf disports itself, and leaves its stall, and so Ephraim was untrained like a calf far away from the stall; because he had forsaken the stall of the Lord, followed Jeroboam, [3095] and worshipped the calves, which future event was prophetically indicated through Aaron, [3096]

namely, that the people of the Jews would fall after this manner. And so repenting, Ephraim says: "Turn Thou me, and I shall be turned, for Thou art the Lord my God. Surely in the end of my captivity I repented, and after I learned I mourned over the days of confusion, and subjected myself to Thee because I received reproach and made Thee known." [3097]

37. We see how to repent, with what words and with what acts, that the days of sin are called "days of confusion;" for there is confusion when Christ is denied.

38. Let us, then, submit ourselves to God, and not be subject to sin, and when we ponder the remembrance of our offences, let us blush as though at some disgrace, and not speak of them as a glory to us, as some boast of overcoming modesty, or putting down the feeling of justice. Let our conversion be such, that we who did not know God may now ourselves declare Him to others, that the Lord, moved by such a conversion on our part, may answer to us: "Ephraim is from youth a dear son, a pleasant child, for since My words are concerning him, I will verily remember him, therefore have I hastened to be over him; I will surely have mercy on him, saith the Lord." [3098]

39. And what mercy He promises us, the Lord also shows, when He says further on: "I have satiated every thirsty soul, and have satisfied every hungry soul. Therefore, I awaked and beheld, and My sleep was sweet unto Me." [3099] We observe that the Lord promises His sacraments to those who sin. Let us, then, all be converted to the Lord.

[3086] S. Matt. viii. 19, 20.

[3087] Jer. xxvi. 2, 3.

113

[3088] Ezek. ii. 4, 5.

[3089] Hom. Il. III. 408. St. Ambrose is hardly right in assuming that Homer used tacha with the sense of "perchance," though this is common in later Greek. In Homer it means quickly.

[3090] S. Matt. xxi. 37.

[3091] S. John viii. 19.

[3092] Ps. xxxii. [xxxi.] 1, 2.

[3093] Jer. xxxi. 18.

[3094] Jer. xxxi. 18.

[3095] Ecclus. xlvii. 23.

[3096] Ex. xxxi.

[3097] Jer. xxxi. 19 [very loosely].

[3098] Jer. xxxi. [LXX.] 20.

[3099] Jer. xxxi. 25, 26.

Chapter VI.
St. Ambrose teaches out of the prophet Isaiah what they must do who have fallen. Then referring to our Lord's proverbial expression respecting piping and dancing, he condemns dances. Next by the example of Jeremiah he sets forth the necessary accompaniments of repentance. And lastly, in order to show the efficacy of this medicine of penance, he enumerates the names of many who have used it for themselves or for others.

40. But if they be not converted, do you at least repent, who by many a slip have fallen from the lofty pinnacle of innocence and faith. We have a good Lord, Whose will it is to forgive all, Who called you by the prophet and said: "I, even I, am He that blotteth out thy transgressions, and I will not remember, but do thou remember that we may plead together." "I," He says, "will not remember, but do thou remember," that is to say, "I do not recall those transgressions which I have forgiven thee, which are covered, as it were, with oblivion, but do thou remember them. I will not remember them because of My grace, do thou remember them in order to correction; remember, thou mayest know that the sin is forgiven, boast not as though innocent, that thou aggravate not the sin, but thou wilt be justified, confess thy sin." For a shamefaced confession of sins looses the bands of transgression.

41. You see what God requires of you, that you remember that grace which you have received, and boast not as though you had not received it. You see by how complete a promise of remission He draws you to confession. Take heed, lest by resisting the commandments of God you fall into the offence of the Jews, to whom the Lord Jesus said: "We piped to you and ye danced not; we wailed and ye wept not." [3100]

42. The words are ordinary words, but the mystery is not ordinary. And so one must be on one's guard, lest, deceived by any common interpretation of this saying, one should suppose that the movements of wanton dances and the madness of the stage were commended; for these are full of evil in youthful age. But the dancing is commended which David practised before the ark of God. For everything is seemly which is done for religion, so that we need be ashamed of no service which tends to the worship and honouring of Christ.

43. Dancing, then, which is an accompaniment of pleasures and luxury, is not spoken of, but spiritually such as that wherewith one raises the eager body, and suffers not the limbs to lie slothfully on the ground, nor to grow stiff in their accustomed tracks. Paul danced spiritually, when for us he stretched forward, and forgetting the things which were behind, and aiming at those which were before, he pressed on to the prize of Christ. [3101] And you, too, when you come to baptism, are warned to raise the hands, and to cause your feet wherewith you ascend to things eternal to be swifter. This dancing accompanies faith, and is the companion of grace.

44. This, then, is the mystery. "We piped to you," singing in truth the song of the New Testament, "and ye danced not." That is, did not raise your souls to the spiritual grace. "We wailed, and ye wept not." That is, ye did not repent. And therefore was the Jewish people forsaken, because it did not repent, and rejected grace. Repentance came by John, grace by Christ. He, as the Lord, gives the one; the other is proclaimed, as it were, by the servant. The Church, then, keeps both that it may both attain to grace and not cast away repentance, for grace is the gift of One Who confers it; repentance is the remedy of the sinner.

45. Jeremiah knew that penitence was a great remedy, which he in his Lamentations took up for Jerusalem, and brings forward Jerusalem itself as repenting, when he says: "She wept sore in the night, and her tears are on her cheeks, nor is there one to comfort her of all who love her. The ways of Sion do mourn." [3102] And he says further: "For these things I weep, my eyes have grown dim with weeping, because he who used to comfort me is gone far from me." [3103] We notice that he thought this the bitterest addition to his woes, that he who used to comfort the mourner was gone far from him. How, then, can you take away the very comfort by refusing to repentance the hope of forgiveness?

46. But let those who repent learn how they ought to carry it out, with what zeal, with what affection, with what intention of mind, with what shaking of the inmost bowels, with what conversion of heart: "Behold," he says, "O Lord, that I am in distress, my bowels are troubled by my weeping, my heart is turned within me." [3104]

47. Here you recognize the intention of the soul, the faithfulness of the mind, the disposition of the body: "The elders of the daughters of Sion sat," he says, "upon the ground, they put dust upon their heads, they girded themselves with haircloth, the princes hung their heads to the ground, the virgins of Jerusalem fainted with weeping, my eyes grew dim, my bowels were troubled, my glory was poured on the earth." [3105]

48. So, too, did the people of Nineveh mourn, and escaped the destruction of their city. [3106] Such is the remedial power of repentance, that God seems because of it to change His intention. To escape is, then, in your own power; the Lord wills

to be entreated, He wills that men should hope in Him, He wills that supplication should be made to Him. Thou art a man, and willest to be asked to forgive, and dost thou think that God will pardon thee without asking Him?

49. The Lord Himself wept over Jerusalem, that, inasmuch as it would not weep itself, it might obtain forgiveness through the tears of the Lord. He wills that we should weep in order that we may escape, as you find it in the Gospel: "Daughters of Jerusalem, weep not for Me, but weep for yourselves." [3107]

50. David wept, and obtained of the divine mercy the removal of the death of the people who were perishing, when of the three things proposed for his choice he selected that in which he might have the most experience of the divine mercy. Why do you blush to weep for your sins, when God commanded even the prophets to weep for the people?

51. And, lastly, Ezekiel was bidden to weep for Jerusalem, and he took the book, at the beginning of which was written: "Lamentation, and melody, and woe," [3108] two things sad and one pleasant, for he shall be saved in the future who has wept most in this age. "For the heart of the wise is in the house of mourning, and the heart of fools in the house of feasting." [3109] And the Lord Himself said: "Blessed are ye that weep now, for ye shall laugh." [3110]

[3100] S. Luke vii. 32.

[3101] Phil. ii. 13, 14.

[3102] Lam. i. 2, 4.

[3103] Lam. i. 16.

[3104] Lam. i. 20.

[3105] Lam. ii. 10, 11.

[3106] Jon. iii. 5.

[3107] S. Luke xxiii. 28.

[3108] Ezek. ii. 9 [LXX.].

[3109] Eccles. vii. 4.

[3110] S. Luke vi. 21.

Chapter VII.

An exhortation to mourning and confession of sins for Christ is moved by these and the tears of the Church. Illustration from the story of Lazarus. After showing that the Novatians are the successors of those who planned to kill Lazarus, St. Ambrose argues that the full forgiveness of every sin is signified by the odour of the ointment poured by Mary on the feet of Christ; and further, that the Novatian heretics find their likeness in Judas, who grudged and envied when others rejoiced.

52. Let us, then, mourn for a time, that we may rejoice for eternity. Let us fear the Lord, let us anticipate Him with the confession of our sins, let us correct our backslidings and amend our faults, lest of us too it be said: "Woe is me, my soul, for the godly man is perished from the earth, and there is none amongst men to correct them." [3111]

53. Why do you fear to confess your sins to our good Lord? "Set them forth," He says, "that thou mayest be justified." The rewards of justification are set before him who is still guilty of sin, for he is justified who voluntarily confesses his own sin; and lastly, "the just man is his own accuser in the beginning of

119

his speaking." [3112] The Lord knows all things, but He waits for your words, not that He may punish, but that He may pardon. It is not His will that the devil should triumph over you and accuse you when you conceal your sins. Be beforehand with your accuser: if you accuse yourself, you will fear no accuser; if you report yourself, though you were dead you shall live.

54. Christ will come to your grave, and if He finds there weeping for you Martha the woman of good service, and Mary who carefully heard the Word of God, like holy Church which has chosen the best part, He will be moved with compassion, when at your death He shall see the tears of many and will say: "Where have ye laid him?" [3113] that is to say, in what condition of guilt is he? in which rank of penitents? I would see him for whom ye weep, that he himself may move Me with his tears. I will see if he is already dead to that sin for which forgiveness is entreated.

55. The people will say to Him, "Come and see." [3114] What is the meaning of "Come"? It means, Let forgiveness of sins come, let the life of the departed come, the resurrection of the dead, let Thy kingdom come to this sinner also.

56. He will come and will command that the stone be taken away which his fall has laid on the shoulders of the sinner. He could have removed the stone by a word of command, for even inanimate nature is wont to obey the bidding of Christ. He could by the silent power of His working have removed the stone of the sepulchre, at Whose Passion the stones being suddenly removed many sepulchres of the dead were opened, but He bade men remove the stone, in very truth indeed, that the unbelieving might believe what they saw, and see the dead

rising again, but in a type that He might give us the power of lightening the burden of sins, the heavy pressure as it were upon the guilty. Ours it is to remove the burdens, His to raise again, His to bring forth from the tombs those set free from their bands.

57. So the Lord Jesus, seeing the heavy burden of the sinner, weeps, for the Church alone He suffers not to weep. He has compassion with His beloved, and says to him that is dead, "Come forth," [3115] that is, Thou who liest in darkness of conscience, and in the squalor of thy sins, as in the prison-house of the guilty, come forth, declare thy sins that thou mayest be justified. "For with the mouth confession is made unto salvation." [3116]

58. If you have confessed at the call of Christ the bars will be broken, and every chain loosed, even the stench of the bodily corruption be grievous. For he had been dead four days and his flesh stank in the tomb; but He Whose flesh saw no corruption was three days in the sepulchre, for He knew no evils of the flesh, which consists of the substances of the four elements. However great, then, the stench of the dead body may be, it is all done away so soon as the sacred ointment has shed its odour; and the dead rises again, and the command is given to loose his hands who till now was in sin; the covering is taken from his face which veiled the truth of the grace which he had received. But since he has received forgiveness, the command is given to uncover his face, to lay bare his features. For he whose sin is forgiven has nothing whereof to be ashamed.

59. But in the presence of such grace given by the Lord, of such a miracle of divine bounty, when all ought to have rejoiced, the wicked were stirred up and gathered a council

against Christ, [3117] and wished moreover to kill Lazarus also. [3118] Do you not recognize that you are the successors of those whose hardness you inherit? For you too are angry and gather a council against the Church, because you see the dead come to life again in the Church, and to be raised again by receiving forgiveness of their sins. And thus, so far as in you, you desire to slay again through envy those who are raised to life.

60. But Jesus does not revoke His benefits, nay, rather He amplifies them by additions of His liberality, He anxiously revisits him who was raised again, and rejoicing in the gift of the restored life, He comes to the feast which His Church has prepared for Him, at which he who had been dead is found as one amongst those sitting down with Christ.

61. Then all wonder who look upon him with the pure gaze of the mind, who are free from envy, for such children the Church has. They wonder, as I said, how he who yesterday and the day before lay in the tomb is one of those sitting with the Lord Jesus.

62. Mary herself pours ointment on the feet of the Lord Jesus. [3119] Perchance for this reason on His feet, because one of the lowliest has been snatched from death, for we are all the body of Christ, [3120] but others perchance are the more honourable members. The Apostle was the mouth of Christ, for he said, "Ye seek a proof of Christ that speaketh in me." [3121] The prophets through whom He spake of things to come were His mouth, would that I might be found worthy to be His foot, and may Mary pour on me her precious ointment, and anoint me and wipe away my sin.

63. What, then, we read concerning Lazarus we ought to believe of every sinner who is converted, who, though he may have been stinking, nevertheless is cleansed by the precious ointment of faith. For faith has such grace that there where the dead stank the day before, now the whole house is filled with good odour.

64. The house of Corinth stank, when it was written concerning it: "It is reported that there is fornication among you, and such fornication as is not even among the Gentiles." [3122] There was a stench, for a little leaven had corrupted the whole lump. A good odour began when it was said: "If ye forgive anything to any one I forgive also. For what I also have forgiven, for your sakes have I done it in the person of Christ." [3123] And so, the sinner being set free, there was great joy in that place, and the whole house was filled with the odour of the sweetness of grace. Wherefore the Apostle, knowing well that he had shed upon all the ointment of apostolic forgiveness, says: "We are a sweet savour of Christ unto God in them that are saved." [3124]

65. At the pouring forth, then, of this ointment all rejoice; Judas alone speaks against it. [3125] So, too, now he who is a sinner speaks against it, he who is a traitor blames it, but he is himself blamed by Christ, as he knows not the remedy of the Lord's death, and understands not the mystery of that so great burial. For the Lord both suffered and died that He might redeem us from death. This is manifest from the most excellent value from His death, which is sufficient for the absolution of the sinner, and his restoration to fresh grace; so that all may come and wonder at his sitting at table with Christ, and may praise God, saying: "Let us eat and feast, for he was dead and is alive again, had perished and is found." [3126] But any one

devoid of faith objects: "Why does He eat with publicans and sinners?" This is his answer: "They that are whole have no need of the physician, but they that are sick." [3127]

[3111] Mic. vii. 2 [LXX.].

[3112] Prov. xviii. 17.

[3113] S. John xi. 34.

[3114] S. John xi. 34.

[3115] S. John xi. 43.

[3116] Rom. x. 10.

[3117] S. John xi. 47.

[3118] S. John xii. 10.

[3119] S. John xii. 3.

[3120] 1 Cor. xii. 27.

[3121] 2 Cor. xiii. 3.

[3122] 1 Cor. v. 1.

[3123] 2 Cor. ii. 10.

[3124] 2 Cor. ii. 15.

[3125] S. John xii. 4.

[3126] S. Luke xv. 24.

[3127] S. Matt. ix. 11, 12.

Chapter VIII.
In urging repentance St. Ambrose turns to his own case,
expressing the wish that he could wash our Lord's feet like the
woman in the Gospel, which is a great pattern of penitence,
though such as cannot attain to it find acceptance. He prays for
himself, especially that he may sorrow with sinners, who are
better than himself. Those for whom Christ died are not to be
contemned.

66. Show, then, your wound to the Physician that He may heal it. Though you show it not, He knows it, but waits to hear your voice. Do away your scars by tears. Thus did that woman in the Gospel, and wiped out the stench of her sin; thus did she wash away her fault, when washing the feet of Jesus with her tears.

67. Would that Thou, Lord Jesus, mightest reserve for me the washing off from Thy feet of the stains contracted since Thou walkest in me! O that Thou mightest offer to me to cleanse the pollution which I by my deeds have caused on Thy steps! But whence can I obtain living water, wherewith I may wash Thy feet? If I have no water I have tears, and whilst with them I wash Thy feet I trust to cleanse myself. Whence is it that Thou shouldst say to me: "His sins which are many are forgiven, because he loved much"? I confess that I owe more, and that more has been forgiven me who have been called to the priesthood from the tumult and strife of the law courts and the dread of public administration; and therefore I fear that I may be found ungrateful, if I, to whom more has been forgiven, love less.

68. But all are not able to equal that woman, who was deservedly preferred even to Simon, who was giving the feast to the Lord; who gave a lesson to all who desire to gain forgiveness, by kissing the feet of Christ, washing them with

her tears, wiping them with her hair, and anointing them with ointment.

69. In a kiss is the sign of love, and therefore the Lord Jesus says: "Let her kiss Me with the kisses of her mouth." [3128] What is the meaning of the hair, but that you may learn that, having laid aside all the pomp of worldly trappings, you must implore pardon, throw yourself on the earth with tears, and prostrate on the ground move pity. In the ointment, too, is set forth the savour of a good conversation. David was a king, yet he said: "Every night will I wash my bed, I will water my couch with tears." [3129] And therefore he obtained such a favour, as that of his house the Virgin should be chosen, who by her child-bearing should bring forth Christ for us. Therefore is this woman also praised in the Gospel.

70. Nevertheless if we are unable to equal her, the Lord Jesus knows also how to aid the weak, when there is no one who can prepare the feast, or bring the ointment, or carry with her a spring of living water. He comes Himself to the sepulchre.

71. Would that Thou wouldst vouchsafe to come to this sepulchre of mine, O Lord Jesus, that Thou wouldst wash me with Thy tears, since in my hardened eyes I possess not such tears as to be able to wash away my offence. If Thou shalt weep for me I shall be saved; if I am worthy of Thy tears I shall cleanse the stench of all my offences; if I am worthy that Thou weep but a little, Thou wilt call me out of the tomb of this body and will say: "Come forth," that my meditations may not be kept pent up in the narrow limits of this body, but may go forth to Christ, and move in the light, that I may think no more on works of darkness but on works of light. For he who thinks on

sins endeavours to shut himself up within his own consciousness.

72. Call forth, then, Thy servant. Although bound with the chain of my sins I have my feet fastened and my hands tied; being now buried in dead thoughts and works, yet at Thy call I shall go forth free, and shall be found one of those sitting at Thy feast, and Thy house shall be filled with precious ointment. If Thou hast vouchsafed to redeem any one, Thou wilt preserve him. For it shall be said, "See, he was not brought up in the bosom of the Church, nor trained from childhood, but hurried from the judgment-seat, brought away from the vanities of this world, growing accustomed to the singing of the choir instead of the shout of the crier, but he continues in the priesthood not by his own strength, but by the grace of Christ, and sits among the guests at the heavenly table.

73. Preserve, O Lord, Thy work, guard the gift which Thou hast given even to him who shrank from it. For I knew that I was not worthy to be called a bishop, because I had devoted myself to this world, but by Thy grace I am what I am. And I am indeed the least of all bishops, and the lowest in merit; yet since I too have undertaken some labour for Thy holy Church, watch over this fruit, and let not him whom when lost Thou didst call to the priesthood, to be lost when a priest. And first grant that I may know how with inmost affection to mourn with those who sin; for this is a very great virtue, since it is written: "And thou shalt not rejoice over the children of Judah in the day of their destruction, and speak not proudly in the day of their trouble." [3130] Grant that so often as the sin of any one who has fallen is made known to me I may suffer with him, and not chide him proudly, but mourn and weep, so that

weeping over another I may mourn for myself, saying, "Tamar hath been more righteous than I." [3131]

74. Perchance a maiden may have fallen, deceived and hurried away by those occasions which are the sources of sins. Well, we who are older sin, too. In us, too, the law of this flesh wars against the law of our mind, and makes us captives of sin, so that we do what we would not. [3132] Her youth is an excuse for her, I now have none, for she ought to learn, we ought to teach. So that "Tamar hath been more righteous than I."

75. We inveigh against some one's covetousness, let us call to mind whether we ourselves have never done anything covetously; and if we have, since covetousness is the root of all evils, and is working in our bodies like a serpent secretly under the earth, let each of us say: "Tamar hath been more righteous than I."

76. If we have been seriously moved against any one, a layman may act hastily for a smaller matter than a bishop. Let us ponder that with ourselves and say, He who is reproved for quick temper is more righteous than I. For if we thus speak, we guard ourselves against this, that the Lord Jesus or one of His disciples should say to us: "Thou beholdest the mote in thy brother's eye, but beholdest not the beam which is in thine own eye. Thou hypocrite, cast out first the beam out of thine own eye, and then shalt thou see to cast out the mote out of thy brother's eye." [3133]

77. Let us, then, not be ashamed to say that our fault is more serious than that of him whom we think we must reprove, for this is what Judah did who reprimanded Tamar, and remembering his own fault said: "Tamar is more righteous than I." In which saying there is a deep mystery and a moral precept;

and therefore is his offence not reckoned to him, because he accused himself before he was accused by others.

78. Let us, then, not rejoice over the sin of any one, but rather let us mourn, for it is written: "Rejoice not against me, O my enemy, because I have fallen, for I shall arise; for if I sit in darkness the Lord shall be a light unto me, I will bear the indignation of the Lord, because I have sinned against Him, until He maintain my cause, and execute judgment for me, and bring me forth to the light, and I shall behold His righteousness. Mine enemy, too, shall see it and shall be covered with confusion, which said unto me, Where is the Lord thy God? Mine eyes shall behold her, and she shall be for treading down as the mire in the streets." [3134] And this not unreservedly, for he who rejoices at the fall of another rejoices at the victory of the devil. Let us, then, rather mourn when we hear that one has perished for whom Christ died, Who despises not even the straw in time of harvest.

79. O that He may not cast away this straw at His harvest, the empty stalks of my produce; but may He gather it in, as is said by some one: "Woe is me, for I am become as one that gathereth straw in harvest, and grape gleanings in the vintage," [3135] that He may eat of the firstfruits at least of His grace in me, though He approve not the later fruit.

[3128] Cant. i. 2.

[3129] Ps. vi. 6.

[3130] Obad. 12.

[3131] Gen. xxxviii. 26.

[3132] Rom. vii. 23 ff.

[3133] S. Matt. vii. 4, 5.

[3134] Mic. vii. 8, 9, 10.

[3135] Mic. vii. 1.

Chapter IX.
In what way faith is necessary for repentance. Means for paying our debts, in which work, prayer, tears, and fasting are of more value than money. Some instances are adduced, and St. Ambrose declares that generosity is profitable, but only when joined with faith; it is, moreover, liable to certain defects. He goes on to speak of some defects in repentance, such as too great haste in seeking reconciliation, considering abstinence from sacraments all that is needed, of committing sin in hope of repenting later.

80. So, then, it is fitting for us to believe both that sinners must repent and that forgiveness is to be given on repentance, yet still as hoping for forgiveness as granted upon faith, not as a debt, for it is one thing to earn, and another presumptuously to claim a right. Faith asks for forgiveness, as it were, by covenant, but presumption is more akin to demand than to request. Pay first that which you owe, that you may be in a position to ask for what you have hoped. Come with the disposition of an honest debtor, that you may not contract a fresh liability, but may pay that which is due of the existing debt with the possessions of your faith.

81. He who owes a debt to God has more help towards payment than he who is indebted to man. Man requires money for money, and this is not always at the debtor's command. God demands the affection of the heart, which is in our own power. No one who owes a debt to God is poor, except one who has made himself poor. And even if he have nothing to

sell, yet has he wherewith to pay. Prayer, fasting, and tears are the resources of an honest debtor, and much more abundant than if one from the price of his estate offered money without faith.

82. Ananias was poor, when after selling his land he brought the money to the apostles, and was not able with it to pay his debt, but involved himself the more. [3136] That widow was rich who cast her two small pieces into the treasury, of whom Christ said: "This poor widow hath cast in more than they all." [3137] For God requires not money but faith.

83. And I do not deny that sins may be diminished by liberal gifts to the poor, but only if faith commend what is spent. For what would the giving of one's whole property benefit without charity?

84. There are some who aim at the credit of generosity for pride alone, because they wish thereby to gain the good opinion of the multitude for leaving nothing to themselves; but whilst they are seeking rewards in this life, they are laying up none for the life to come, and having received their reward here they cannot hope for it there.

85. Some again, having, through impulsive excitement and not after long consideration, given their possessions to the Church, think that they can claim them back. These gain neither the first nor the second reward, for the gift was made thoughtlessly, its recall sacrilegiously.

86. Some repent of having distributed their property to the poor. But they who are doing penance must not repent of this, lest they repent of their own repentance. For many seek for penance through fear of future punishment, being conscious of

their sins, and having received their penance are held back by fear of the public entreaties. These persons seem to have sought for repentance for their evil deeds, but to exercise it for their good ones.

87. Some seek penance because they wish to be at once restored to communion. These wish not so much to loose themselves as to bind the priest, for they do not put off the guilt from their own conscience, but lay it on that of the priest, to whom the command is given: "Give not that which is holy to the dogs, neither cast your pearls before the swine;" [3138] that is to say, that partaking of the holy Communion is not to be allowed to those polluted with impurity.

88. And so one may see those walking in other attire, who ought to be weeping and groaning because they had defiled the robe of sanctification and grace; and women loading their ears with pearls, and weighing down their necks, who had better have bent to Christ than to gold, and who ought to be weeping for themselves, because they have lost the pearl from heaven.

89. There are, again, some who think that it is penitence to abstain from the heavenly sacraments. These are too cruel judges of themselves, who prescribe a penalty for themselves but refuse the remedy, who ought to be mourning over their self-imposed penalty, because it deprives them of heavenly grace.

90. Others think that licence is granted them to sin, because the hope of penitence is before them, whereas penitence is the remedy, not an incentive to sin. For the salve is necessary for the wound, not the wound for the salve, since a salve is sought because of the wound, the wound is not wished for on account of the salve. The hope which is put off to a future season is but

feeble, for every season is uncertain, and hope does not outlive all time.

[3136] Acts v. 1, 2.

[3137] S. Luke xxi. 3.

[3138] S. Matt. vii. 6.

Chapter X.

In order to do away with the feeling of shame which holds back the guilty from public penance, St. Ambrose points out the advantage of prayers offered by the whole Church, and sets forth the example of saints who have sorrowed. Then, after reproving those who imagine that penance may be often repeated, he points out the difficulty of repentance, and how it is to be carried out.

91. Can any one endure that you should blush to entreat God, when you do not blush to entreat a man? That you should be ashamed to entreat Him Who knows you fully, when you are not ashamed to confess your sins to a man who knows you not? [3139] Do you shrink from witnesses and sympathizers in your prayers, when, if you have to satisfy a man, you must visit many and entreat them to be kind enough to intervene; when you throw yourself at a man's knees, kiss his feet, bring your children, still unconscious of guilt, to entreat also for their father's pardon? And you disdain to do this in the Church in order to entreat God, in order to gain for yourself the support of the holy congregation; where there is no cause for shame, except indeed not to confess, since we are all sinners, amongst whom he is the most praiseworthy who is the most humble; he is the most just who feels himself the lowest.

92. Let the Church, our Mother, weep for you, and wash away your guilt with her tears; let Christ see you mourning and say, "Blessed are ye that are sad, for ye shall rejoice." It pleases Him that many should entreat for one. In the Gospel, too, moved by the widow's tears, because many were weeping for her, He raised her son. He heard Peter more quickly when He raised Dorcas, because the poor were mourning over the death of the woman. He also forthwith forgave Peter, for he wept most bitterly. And if you weep bitterly Christ will look upon you and your guilt shall leave you. For the application of pain does away with the enjoyment of the wickedness and the delight of the sin. And so while mourning over our past sins we shut the door against fresh ones, and from the condemnation of our guilt there arises as it were a training in innocence.

93. Let, then, nothing call you away from penitence, for this you have in common with the saints, and would that such sorrowing for sin as that of the saints were copied by you. David, as it were, "ate ashes for bread, and mingled his drink with weeping," [3140] and therefore now rejoices the more because he wept the more: "Mine eyes ran down," he said, "with rivers of water." [3141]

94. John wept sore, [3142] and, as he tells us, the mysteries of Christ were revealed to him. But that woman who, when she was in sin and ought to have wept, nevertheless rejoiced, and covered herself with a robe of purple and scarlet, [3143] and adorned herself with much gold and precious stones, now mourns the misery of eternal weeping.

95. Deservedly are they blamed who think that they often do penance, for they are wanton against Christ. For if they went through their penance in truth, they would not think that it

could be repeated again; for as there is but one baptism, so there is but one course of penance, so far as the outward practice goes, for we must repent of our daily faults, but this latter has to do with lighter faults, the former with such as are graver.

96. But I have more easily found such as had preserved their innocence than such as had fittingly repented. Does any one think that that is penitence where there still exists the striving after earthly honours, where wine flows, and even conjugal connection takes place? The world must be renounced; less sleep must be indulged in than nature demands; it must be broken by groans, interrupted by sighs, put aside by prayers; the mode of life must be such that we die to the usual habits of life. Let the man deny himself and be wholly changed, as in the fable they relate of a certain youth, who left his home because of his love for a harlot, and, having subdued his love, returned; then one day meeting his old favourite and not speaking to her, she, being surprised and supposing that he had not recognized her, said, when they met again, "It is I." "But," was his answer, "I am not the former I."

97. Well then did the Lord say: "If any man will come after Me, let him deny himself, and take up his cross and follow Me." [3144] For they who are dead and buried in Christ ought not again to make their conclusions as though living in the world. "Touch not," it is said, "nor attend to those things which tend to corruption by their very use, [3145] for the very customs of this life corrupt integrity."

[3139] A good deal of controversy has arisen about this passage, which certainly appears, prima facie, to contrast confession to God and to a man obviously priest or bishop.

The Benedictine editors insist much upon the use of the singular number, homini, a man. But the word might conceivably be used in a general sense. There is no real doubt as to the practice of the Early Church. See note at the end of this treatise.

[3140] Ps. cii. [ci.] 9.

[3141] Ps. cxix. [cxviii.] 136.

[3142] Rev. v. 4.

[3143] Rev. xvii. 4.

[3144] S. Matt. xvi. 24.

[3145] Col. ii. 21. We have here an instance of a very extreme kind, of the way in which St. Ambrose and other writers occasionally quote the words of holy Scripture without reference to their context or real meaning. The words suit the argument of St. Ambrose and he uses them. But they mean almost the very opposite in the original. They are part of the argument which St. Paul is opposing, not his argument.

Chapter XI.
The possibility of repentance is a reason why baptism should not be deferred to old age, a practice which is against the will of God in holy Scripture. But it is of no use to practise penance whilst still serving lusts. These must be first subdued.

98. Good, then, is penitence, and if there were no place for it, every one would defer the grace of cleansing by baptism to old age. And a sufficient reason is that it is better, to have a robe to mend, than none to put on; but as that which has been repaired

once is restored, so that which is frequently mended is destroyed.

99. And the Lord has given a sufficient warning to those who put off repentance, when He says: "Repent ye, for the kingdom of heaven is at hand." [3146] We know not at what hour the thief will come, we know not whether our soul may be required of us this next night. God cast Adam out of Paradise immediately after his fault; there was no delay. At once the fallen were severed from all their enjoyments that they might do penance; at once God clothed them with garments of skins, not of silk. [3147]

100. And what reason is there for putting off? Is it that you may sin yet more? Then because God is good you are evil, and "despise the riches of His goodness and long-suffering." [3148] But the goodness of the Lord ought rather to draw you to repentance. Wherefore holy David says to all: "Come, let us worship and fall down before Him, and mourn before our Lord Who made us." [3149] But for a sinner who has died without repentance, because nothing remains but to mourn grievously and to weep, you find him groaning and saying: "O my son Absalom! my son Absalom!" [3150] For him who is wholly dead mourning is without alleviation.

101. But of those who as exiles and banished from their ancestral homes, which the holy law of Moses had assigned them, will be entangled in the errors of the world, you hear him saying: "By the waters of Babylon we sat down and wept, when we remembered Zion." [3151] He sets forth the wailings of those who have fallen, and shows that they who are living in this condition of passing time and changing circumstances

ought to repent, after the example of those who, as a reward for sin, had been led into miserable captivity.

102. But nothing causes such exceeding grief as when any one, lying under the captivity of sin, calls to mind whence he has fallen, because he turned aside to carnal and earthly things, instead of directing his mind in the beautiful ways of the knowledge of God.

103. So you find Adam concealing himself, when he knew that God was present, and wishing to be hidden when called by God with that voice which wounded the soul of him who was hiding: "Adam, where art thou?" [3152] That is to say, Wherefore hidest thou thyself? Why art thou concealed? Why dost thou avoid Him, Whom thou once didst long to see? A guilty conscience is so burdensome that it punishes itself without a judge, and wishes for covering, and yet is bare before God.

104. And so no one in a state of sin ought to claim a right to or the use of the sacraments, for it is written: "Thou hast sinned, be still." [3153] As David says in the Psalm lately quoted: "We hanged our harps upon the willows in the midst thereof;" and again: "How shall we sing the Lord's song in a strange land?" [3154] For if the flesh wars against the mind, and is not subject to the guidance of the Spirit, that is a strange land which is not subdued by the toil of the cultivator, and so cannot produce the fruits of charity, patience, and peace. It is better, then, to be still when you cannot practise the works of repentance, lest in the very acts of repentance there be that which afterward will need further repentance. For if it be once entered upon and not rightly carried out, it obtains not the result of a first repentance and takes away the use of a later one. [3155]

105. When, then, the flesh resists, the soul must be intent upon God, and if results do not follow, let not faith fail. And if the enticements of the flesh come upon us, or the powers of the enemy attack us, let the soul keep in submission to God. For we are then specially oppressed when the flesh yields. And some there are who trouble heavily the wretched soul, seeking to deprive it of all protection. To which case the words apply: "Rase it, rase it, even to the foundations." [3156]

106. And David, pitying her, says: "O wretched daughter of Babylon." [3157] Wretched indeed, as being the daughter of Babylon, when she ceased to be the daughter of Jerusalem. [3158] And yet he calls for a healer for her, and says: "Blessed is he who shall take thy little ones and dash them against the rock." [3159] That is to say, shall dash all corrupt and filthy thoughts against Christ, Who by His fear and His rebuke will break down all motions against reason, so as, if any one is seized by an adulterous love, to extinguish the fire, that he may by his zeal put away the love of a harlot, and deny himself that he may gain Christ.

107. We have then learned that we must do penance, and this at a time when the heat of luxury and sin is giving way; and that we, when under the dominion of sin, must show ourselves Godfearing by refraining, rather than allowing ourselves in evil practices. For if it is said to Moses when he was desiring to draw nearer: "Put off thy shoes from off thy feet," [3160] how much more must we free the feet of our soul from the bonds of the body, and clear our steps from all connection with this world.

[3146] S. Matt. iv. 17.

[3147] Gen. iii. 21, 24.

[3148] Rom. ii. 4.

[3149] Ps. xcv. [xciv.] 6.

[3150] 2 Sam. [2 Kings] xviii. 33.

[3151] Ps. cxxxvii. [cxxxvi.] 1.

[3152] Gen. iii. 9.

[3153] Gen. iv. 7 [LXX.]. These words occur in the Septuagint only, and would seem to be taken here by St. Ambrose as a warning from God to Cain, not to sacrifice whilst in sin, and so be applied to those sinners whom he enjoins not to communicate before they repent.

[3154] Ps. cxxxvii. [cxxxvi.] 2, 4.

[3155] I do not feel sure of the meaning of this passage, but it appears to be as above, that a person going through the outward exercises of penance without inward repentance, gains no benefit, and as sinners were not admitted to a second course of penance, does away with his chance for the future. [Ed.]

[3156] Ps. cxxxvii. [cxxxvi.] 7.

[3157] Ps. cxxxvii. [cxxxvi.] 8 [LXX.].

[3158] This passage is another instance of the way in which St. Ambrose, like many other early writers, lost sight of the original meaning of the text in drawing allegorical lessons from it. The "daughter of Babylon," i.e. the people, had never been a "daughter of God," nor was the dashing of the children against the rock ever intended to bear the beautiful interpretation given to it by our author.

[3159] Ps. cxxxvii. [cxxxvi.] 9.

[3160] Ex. iii. 5.

Note on the Penitential Discipline of the Early Church.

It was always believed in the Church that the power of binding and loosing had been entrusted by our Lord to His apostles, and by them handed on to their successors in the ministry. The earlier practice would seem to have been short and simple: exclusion from Communion, some outward discipline, not always continued for a long period, and reconciliation on true repentance, these matters being decided by the bishop at his discretion. Gradually the practice became more systematized, various periods of discipline were prescribed for various sins, and the time for this discipline was lengthened.

There were three parts in the discipline of Penitence as a whole:

1. Confession, exomologesis, a term used frequently of the whole course.

2. Penance, properly so called, i.e. the mortifications, fasting, etc., prescribed.

3. Reconciliation, performed solemnly by the bishop, often at Easter.

The confession was probably in private to the bishop, who determined whether any public confession should be made or not. But as only great sins--at first, idolatry, adultery, and murder (peccata mortalia)--were punished by outward penance, it was clear that the sin must have been very grievous.

The Montanists taught that the Church had not power to forgive great sins, and this led to clearing the doctrine, and from the middle of the third century, even those who had lapsed into idolatry were admitted to penance.

Hermas already says: tois doulois toutheou metanoia esti mia, Mand. iv. 1. And this rule seems to have been maintained as regards the formal penance and reconciliation, not as implying doubt of possible forgiveness, but as a matter of discipline, and this rule deprived those who fell a second time from communion at least till their deathbed.

For this public penance the Greek words are metanoia and exomologesis; the Latin, penitentia and frequently exomologesis. As the word penitentia includes not merely sorrow for sin and change of heart, but also penance, or the penalty inflicted by authority, and is used in such phrases as penitentiam agere or facere, it has been necessary in the translation of the De Penitentia to vary the English terms, and to use sometimes repentance, sometimes penance.

For further information on this subject, the reader is referred specially to the Articles, Buss-Disciplin, in the Freiburg Kirchen-Lexikon, by Wetzer and Welte; and to those on Exomologesis, Penitence, and Reconciliation, in the Dict. of Christian Antiquities, where other authorities and references will be found.

Made in the USA
Middletown, DE
20 August 2024

59512582R00082